# Python Programming with Raspberry Pi

Build small yet powerful robots and automation systems with Raspberry Pi Zero

**Sai Yamanoor**
**Srihari Yamanoor**

BIRMINGHAM - MUMBAI

# Python Programming with Raspberry Pi

First published: April 2017

Production reference: 1270417

Published by Packt Publishing Ltd.
Livery Place
35 Livery Street
Birmingham
B3 2PB, UK.

ISBN 978-1-78646-757-7

www.packtpub.com

# Credits

**Authors**
Sai Yamanoor
Srihari Yamanoor

**Reviewer**
Ian McAlpine

**Commissioning Editor**
Vijin Boricha

**Acquisition Editor**
Rahul Nair

**Content Development Editor**
Abhishek Jadhav

**Technical Editor**
Gaurav Suri

**Copy Editors**
Safis Editing
Dipti Mankame

**Project Coordinator**
Judie Jose

**Proofreader**
Safis Editing

**Indexer**
Pratik Shirodkar

**Graphics**
Kirk D'Penha

**Production Coordinator**
Shantanu N. Zagade

# About the Authors

**Sai Yamanoor** is an embedded systems engineer working for a private startup school in the San Francisco Bay Area, where he builds devices that helps students achieve their full potential. He completed his graduate studies in Mechanical Engineering at Carnegie Mellon University, Pittsburgh PA, and his undergraduate work in Mechatronics Engineering from Sri Krishna College of Engineering and Technology, Coimbatore, India. His interests, deeply rooted in DIY and ppen software and hardware cultures, include developing gadgets and apps that improve Quality of Life, Internet of Things, crowdfunding, education, and new technologies. In his spare time, he plays with various devices and architectures such as the Raspberry Pi, Arduino, Galileo, Android devices and others. Sai blogs about his adventures with Mechatronics at the aptly named *Mechatronics Craze* blog at `http://mechatronicscraze.wordpress.com/`. You can find his project portfolios at `http://saiyamanoor.com`.

This book is Sai's second title and he has earlier published a book titled *Raspberry Pi Mechatronics Projects*.

*I would like to thank my parents for encouraging me in all my endeavors and for making me what I am today. I am thankful to my brother who has helped me shape my career all these years. I would like to sincerely apologize to Balaji Raghavendra for the mixup with the first book and sincerely thank him for his reviews and advice on the first book. I am also thankful to the team at Packt, especially Abhishek who was patient and understanding under trying circumstances.*

**Srihari Yamanoor** is a mechanical engineer, working on medical devices, sustainability, and robotics in the San Francisco Bay Area. He completed his graduate studies in Mechanical Engineering at Stanford University, and his undergraduate studies in Mechanical Engineering from PSG College of Technology, Coimbatore, India. He is severally certified in SolidWorks, Simulation, Sustainable Design, PDM as well as, in quality and reliability engineering and auditing. His interests have a wide range, from DIY, crowdfunding, AI, travelling, and photography to gardening and ecology. In his spare time, he is either traveling across California, dabbling in nature photography, or at home, tinkering with his garden and playing with his cats.

*I have many people to thank for any and all success in my life, one of the culminations being this second book. I start with my parents for always making sure that I put my career and education first. My brother Sai Yamanoor, is the main reason I have my name on not one, but two books! I have to thank several professors and teachers, not the least of whom are Kenneth Waldron, Dr. Radhakrishnan, Dr. R. Rudramoorthy, Dr. K.A. Jagadeesh, Cyril "Master", and the Late "Master" Williams. Of course, I'd be remiss, if I didn't acknowledge my mentors, Russ Sampson, James Stubbs, Mukund Patel, and Anna Tamura. Then, I have my dearest friends, Patrick Nguyen, Anna Jao, Andrew Eib, Vishnu Prasad Ramachandran, and David Ma, who have put up with my quirks over the last several years, patiently offering advice and helping me weather several storms. I too would like to apologize to Balaji Raghavendra, who was left out of the acknowledgements from our last book, purely by accident, and nevertheless, inexcusably so. Without your help, we would not have been able to complete that book and start on this one. I second Sai in recognizing Abhishek Jadhav's immeasurable patience and guidance throughout the course of the publication of this book.  Last but not the least, there are my beloved felines, the glaring that keeps me going – Bob, Gi-Ve, Fish Bone and Saxi.*
*We would like to acknowledge that 100% of the proceeds in revenue and profits of the authors, is being turned over to worthy non-profits.*

# About the Reviewer

**Ian McAlpine** had his first introduction to computers was his school's Research Machines RML-380Z and his physics teacher's Compukit UK101. That was followed by a Sinclair ZX81 and then a BBC Micro Model A, which he still has to this day. That interest resulted in a MEng degree in Electronic Systems Engineering from Aston University and an MSc degree in Information Technology from the University of Liverpool. Ian is currently a Senior Product Expert in the BI & Analytics Competence Centre at SAP Labs in Vancouver, Canada.

The introduction of the Raspberry Pi rekindled his desire to "tinker", but also provided an opportunity to give back to the community. Consequently Ian was a very active volunteer for 3 years on *The MagPi*, a monthly magazine for the Raspberry Pi, which you can read online or download for *free* at `http://www.raspberrypi.org/magpi/`. He also holds an amateur radio license (callsign VE7FTO) and is a communications volunteer for his local community Emergency Management Office. He was a technical reviewer for Packt books, such as *Raspberry Pi Cookbook for Python Programmers*, *Raspberry Pi Projects for Kids*, and *Raspberry Pi 2 Server Essentials*.

*I would like to thank my darling wife, Louise, and my awesome kids Emily and Molly for allowing me to disappear into my "office"…and for training our dog to fetch me!*

# www.PacktPub.com

For support files and downloads related to your book, please visit www.PacktPub.com.

Did you know that Packt offers eBook versions of every book published, with PDF and ePub files available? You can upgrade to the eBook version at www.PacktPub.com and as a print book customer, you are entitled to a discount on the eBook copy. Get in touch with us at service@packtpub.com for more details.

At www.PacktPub.com, you can also read a collection of free technical articles, sign up for a range of free newsletters and receive exclusive discounts and offers on Packt books and eBooks.

https://www.packtpub.com/mapt

Get the most in-demand software skills with Mapt. Mapt gives you full access to all Packt books and video courses, as well as industry-leading tools to help you plan your personal development and advance your career.

# Why subscribe?

- Fully searchable across every book published by Packt
- Copy and paste, print, and bookmark content
- On demand and accessible via a web browser

# Customer Feedback

Thanks for purchasing this Packt book. At Packt, quality is at the heart of our editorial process. To help us improve, please leave us an honest review on this book's Amazon page at `https://www.amazon.com/dp/1786467577`.

If you'd like to join our team of regular reviewers, you can e-mail us at `customerreviews@packtpub.com`. We award our regular reviewers with free eBooks and videos in exchange for their valuable feedback. Help us be relentless in improving our products!

# Table of Contents

# Preface

The Raspberry Pi represents the best in innovation in computer science, education, entertainment, hobby hacking, and several other categories that you can classify the device family into. Even as this book is entering publication, the Raspberry Pi family of products have become the third best selling computers of all time. It is anyone's guess that with the continuing innovation coming out of the Raspberry Pi Foundation and the thousands of people across the planet constantly demonstrating newer and better examples innovative solutions with the various flavors of Raspberry Pi, what new heights this product line might reach!

One of the main goals of the Raspberry Pi is affordability. And the purpose of this book is to allow the beginner to learn Programming in Python, as well as manipulating hardware. The reader may have worked a little bit on hardware, and a little bit on programming, and want to strengthen skills in either area. The reader may also just be interested in doing more projects with the Pi Zero in Python, and of course, some of the projects in this book, briefly highlighted below might be of interest.

The book starts off with some warm up examples, helping develop a familiarity with the Raspberry Pi environment, and the projects increase in variety and complexity as the book progresses. While, readers who have advanced a bit before approaching the book can skip a few chapters, we recommend beginners progress through all chapters, since the concepts build on top of each other.

## What this book covers

Chapter 1, *Getting Started with Python and the Raspberry Pi Zero*, introduces the Raspberry Pi Zero and the Python programming language, its history, and its features. We will set up the Raspberry Pi for Python development and write the first program.

Chapter 2, *Arithmetic Operations, Loops, and Blinky Lights*, walks through the arithmetic operations in Python and loops in Python. In the second half of the chapter, we will discuss the Raspberry Pi Zero's GPIO interface and then learn to blink an LED using a GPIO pin.

Chapter 3, *Conditional Statements, Functions, and Lists*, discusses the types of conditional statements, variables, and logical operators in Python. We will also discuss functions in Python. Then, we will learn to write a function that is used to control DC motors using the Raspberry Pi Zero.

Chapter 4, *Communication Interfaces*, covers all the communication interfaces available on the Raspberry Pi Zero. This includes the I2C, UART, and the SPI interface. These communication interfaces are widely used to interface sensors. Hence, we will demonstrate the operation of each interface using a sensor as an example.

Chapter 5, *Data Types and Object-Oriented Programming in Python*, discusses object-oriented programming in Python and the advantages of object-oriented programming. We will discuss this using a practical example.

Chapter 6, *File I/O and Python Utilities*, discusses reading and writing to files. We discuss creating and updating config files. We will also discuss some utilities available in Python.

Chapter 7, *Requests and Web Frameworks*, discusses libraries and frameworks that enable retrieving data from the Web. We will discuss an example, fetching local weather information. We will also discuss running a web server on the Raspberry Pi Zero.

Chapter 8, *Awesome Things You Could Develop Using Python*, discusses libraries and frameworks that enable retrieving data from the web. We will discuss examples such as fetching the local weather information. We will also discuss running a web server on the Raspberry Pi Zero.

Chapter 9, *Let's Build a Robot!*, shows how we built an indoor robot using the Raspberry Pi Zero as the controller and documented our experience as a step-by-step guide. We wanted to demonstrate the awesomeness of the combination of Python and the Raspberry Pi Zero's peripherals.

Chapter 10, Home Automation Using The Raspberry Pi Zero, discusses four projects, a voice-activated personal assistant, a web framework-based appliance control, a physical activity motivation tool, and a smart lawn sprinkler. Through these projects we provide more examples of the new hardware and programming implementations.

Chapter 11, *Tips and Tricks*, concludes the book with useful hardware and software tips and shortcuts that will help you as you step beyond the concepts and exercises in this book to implement your own projects and solutions, or simply explore the areas of programming and hardware hacking as a hobby and a source of entertainment.

# What you need for this book

The following hardware is recommended:

- A laptop computer, with any OS
- Raspberry Pi Zero
- A microSD card, either 8 GB or 16 GB
- A USB keyboard
- A USB mouse
- A display with HDMI input
- A USB Wi-Fi card
- Power supply, minimum 500 mA.
- Display cables
- Other accessories, as required to complete the various projects in the book

# Who this book is for

This book is primarily aimed at hobbyists and makers. So, some basic exposure to programming, hardware and the Linux OS is assumed. Even without exposure to these areas, it is possible to follow along and benefit from the book. Wherever possible, we have tried our best to point you to free, open and/or cost effective resources to follow along with the projects in the book.

# Conventions

In this book, you will find a number of text styles that distinguish between different kinds of information. Here are some examples of these styles and an explanation of their meaning.

Code words in text, database table names, folder names, filenames, file extensions, pathnames, dummy URLs, user input, and Twitter handles are shown as follows: "The `remove()` method finds the first instance of the element (passed an argument) and removes it from the list."

A block of code is set as follows:

```
try:
    input_value = int(value)
except ValueError as error:
    print("The value is invalid %s" % error)
```

Any command-line input or output is written as follows:

```
sudo pip3 install schedule
```

**New terms** and **important words** are shown in bold. Words that you see on the screen, for example, in menus or dialog boxes, appear in the text like this: "Select the **A8 Serial** option from the drop-down menu."

Warnings or important notes appear in a box like this.

Tips and tricks appear like this.

# Reader feedback

Feedback from our readers is always welcome. Let us know what you think about this book-what you liked or disliked. Reader feedback is important for us as it helps us develop titles that you will really get the most out of.

To send us general feedback, simply e-mail feedback@packtpub.com, and mention the book's title in the subject of your message.

If there is a topic that you have expertise in and you are interested in either writing or contributing to a book, see our author guide at www.packtpub.com/authors.

# Customer support

Now that you are the proud owner of a Packt book, we have a number of things to help you to get the most from your purchase.

# Downloading the example code

You can download the example code files for this book from your account at `http://www.p acktpub.com`. If you purchased this book elsewhere, you can visit `http://www.packtpub.c om/support` and register to have the files e-mailed directly to you.

You can download the code files by following these steps:

1. Log in or register to our website using your e-mail address and password.
2. Hover the mouse pointer on the **SUPPORT** tab at the top.
3. Click on **Code Downloads & Errata**.
4. Enter the name of the book in the **Search** box.
5. Select the book for which you're looking to download the code files.
6. Choose from the drop-down menu where you purchased this book from.
7. Click on **Code Download**.

Once the file is downloaded, please make sure that you unzip or extract the folder using the latest version of:

- WinRAR / 7-Zip for Windows
- Zipeg / iZip / UnRarX for Mac
- 7-Zip / PeaZip for Linux

You can download the latest code samples from the code repository belonging to this book from the author's code repository at `https://github.com/sai-y/pywpi`. You can find additional resources including bonus projects at `http://pywithpi.com`.

The code bundle for the book is also hosted on Packt's GitHub repository at `https://githu b.com/PacktPublishing/Python-Programming-with-Raspberry-Pi-Zero`. We also have other code bundles from our rich catalog of books and videos available at `https://github. com/PacktPublishing/`. Check them out!

# Downloading the color images of this book

We also provide you with a PDF file that has color images of the screenshots/diagrams used in this book. The color images will help you better understand the changes in the output. You can download this file from `https://www.packtpub.com/sites/default/files/down loads/PythonProgrammingwithRaspberryPiZero_ColorImages.pdf`.

# Errata

Although we have taken every care to ensure the accuracy of our content, mistakes do happen. If you find a mistake in one of our books-maybe a mistake in the text or the code- we would be grateful if you could report this to us. By doing so, you can save other readers from frustration and help us improve subsequent versions of this book. If you find any errata, please report them by visiting `http://www.packtpub.com/submit-errata`, selecting your book, clicking on the **Errata Submission Form** link, and entering the details of your errata. Once your errata are verified, your submission will be accepted and the errata will be uploaded to our website or added to any list of existing errata under the Errata section of that title.

To view the previously submitted errata, go to `https://www.packtpub.com/books/content/support`and enter the name of the book in the search field. The required information will appear under the **Errata** section.

# Piracy

Piracy of copyrighted material on the Internet is an ongoing problem across all media. At Packt, we take the protection of our copyright and licenses very seriously. If you come across any illegal copies of our works in any form on the Internet, please provide us with the location address or website name immediately so that we can pursue a remedy.

Please contact us at `copyright@packtpub.com` with a link to the suspected pirated material.

We appreciate your help in protecting our authors and our ability to bring you valuable content.

# Questions

If you have a problem with any aspect of this book, you can contact us at `questions@packtpub.com`, and we will do our best to address the problem.

# 1
# Getting Started with Python and the Raspberry Pi Zero

Over the past few years, the Raspberry Pi family of single board computers has proved to be a revolutionary set of tools for learning, fun, and several serious projects! People over the world are now equipped with the means to learn computer architecture, computer programming, robotics, sensory systems, home automation, and much more, with ease and without blowing a hole in their wallets. This book hopes to help you, the reader, in the journey to learn programming in Python through the **Raspberry Pi Zero**. Among programming languages, Python is simultaneously one of the simplest and easiest to learn as well as one of the most versatile languages. Join us over the next few chapters as we first familiarize ourselves with the Raspberry Pi Zero, a unique and excitingly simple and cheap computer and Python, gradually building projects of increasing challenge and complexity.

In this chapter, we will discuss the following:

- Introduction to the Raspberry Pi Zero and its features
- The setup of the Raspberry Pi Zero
- An introduction to the Python programming language
- The setup of the development environment and writing the first program

## Let's get started!

In the first chapter, we will learn about the Raspberry Pi Zero, set things up for learning Python with this book, and write our first piece of code in Python.

# Things needed for this book

The following items are needed for this book. The sources provided are just a suggestion. The reader is welcome to buy them from an equivalent alternative source:

| Name | Link | Cost (in USD) |
|---|---|---|
| Raspberry Pi Zero (v1.3 or higher) | (The purchase of the Raspberry Pi would be discussed separately) | $5.00 |
| USB hub | `http://amzn.com/B003M0NURK` | $7.00 approx |
| USB OTG cable | `https://www.adafruit.com/products/1099` | $2.50 |
| Micro HDMI to HDMI adapter cable | `https://www.adafruit.com/products/1358` | $6.95 |
| USB Wi-Fi adapter | `http://amzn.com/B00LWE14TO` | $9.45 |
| Micro USB power supply | `http://amzn.com/B00DZLSEVI` | $3.50 |
| Electronics starter kit (or similar) | `http://amzn.com/B00IT6AYJO` | $25.00 |
| 2x20 headers | `https://www.adafruit.com/products/2822` | $0.95 |
| NOOBS micro SD card or a blank 8 GB micro SD card | `http://amzn.com/B00ENPQ1GK` | $13.00 |
| Raspberry Pi camera module (optional) | `http://a.co/6qWiJe6` | $25.00 |
| Raspberry Pi camera adapter (optional) | `https://www.adafruit.com/product/3170` | $5.95 |

The other items needed for this include a USB mouse, USB keyboard, and a monitor with the HDMI output or DVI output. We will also need an HDMI cable (or DVI to HDMI cable if the monitor has an DVI output). Some vendors such as the Pi Hut sell the Raspberry Pi Zero accessories as a kit (for example, `https://thepihut.com/collections/raspberry-pi-accessories/products/raspberry-pi-zero-essential-kit`).

Apart from the components mentioned in this section, we will also discuss certain features of the Raspberry Pi Zero and Python programming using additional components such as sensors and GPIO expanders. These components are optional but definitely useful while learning the different aspects of Python programming.

The electronics starter kit mentioned in the bill of materials is just an example. Feel free to order any beginners electronics kit (that contains a similar mix of electronic components).

# Buying the Raspberry Pi Zero

The Raspberry Pi Zero is sold by distributors such as the **Newark element14**, **Pi Hut**, and **Adafruit**. At the time of writing this book, we encountered difficulties in buying a Raspberry Pi Zero. We recommend monitoring websites such as www.whereismypizero.com to find out when the Raspberry Pi Zero becomes available. We believe that it is rare to locate the Pi Zero because of its popularity. We are not aware if there might be an abundant stock of the Raspberry Pi Zero in the future. The examples discussed in this book are also compatible with the other flavors of the Raspberry Pi (for example, Raspberry Pi 3).

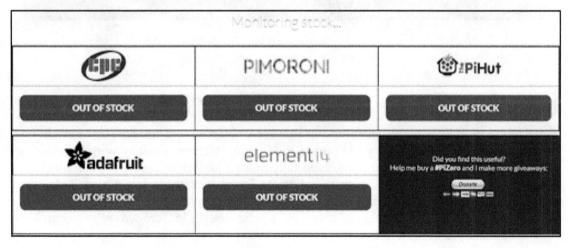

Pi Zero availability information provided by www.whereismypizero.com

While purchasing the Raspberry Pi Zero, make sure that the board version is 1.3 or higher. The board version is printed on the backside of the board (the example of this is shown in the following picture). Verify that the board version using the seller's product description before purchase:

Raspberry Pi board version

# Introduction to the Raspberry Pi Zero

The Raspberry Pi Zero is a small computer that costs about $5 and smaller than a credit card, designed by the **Raspberry Pi Foundation** (a nonprofit organization with the mission to teach computer science to students, especially those who lack of access to the requisite tools). The Raspberry Pi Zero was preceded by the **Raspberry Pi Models A and B**. A detailed history of the Raspberry Pi and the different models of the Raspberry Pi is available on http://elinux.org/RPi_General_History. The Raspberry Pi Zero was released on 26th November 2015 (*Thanksgiving Day*).

A fun fact for the readers is that one of the authors of this book, Sai Yamanoor, drove from San Francisco to Los Angeles (700+ miles for a round trip in one day) on the day after Thanksgiving to buy the Raspberry Pi Zero from a local store.

# The features of the Raspberry Pi Zero

The Raspberry Pi Zero is powered by a 1 GHz BCM2835 processor and 512 MB RAM.
BCM2835 is a **System on a Chip** (**SoC**) developed by Broadcom semiconductors. SoC is one
where all the components required to run a computer are available on a single chip (for
example, the BCM2835 includes CPU, GPU, peripherals such as USB interface). The
documentation for the BCM2835 SoC is available at
`https://www.raspberrypi.org/documentation/hardware/raspberrypi/bcm2835/README.m`
`d`.

The Raspberry Pi Zero board version 1.3

Let's briefly discuss the features of the Raspberry Pi Zero using the preceding picture
marked with numbered rectangles:

1. **The mini HDMI interface**: The mini HDMI interface is used to connect a display
   to the Raspberry Pi Zero. The HDMI interface can be used to drive a display of
   maximum resolution of 1920x1080 pixels.

2. **USB On-The-Go interface**: In the interest of keeping things low cost, the Raspberry Pi Zero comes with a USB **On-The-Group** (**OTG**) interface. This interface enables interfacing USB devices such as a mouse and keyboard. Using a USB OTG to USB-A female converter. We need a USB hub to interface any USB accessory.

3. **Power supply**: The micro-B USB adapter is used to power the Raspberry Pi zero, and it draws about a maximum of 200 mA of current.

4. **micro SD card slot**: The Raspberry Pi's **operating system** (**OS**) resides in a micro SD card and the **bootloader** on the processor loads it upon powering up.

5. **GPIO interface**: The Raspberry Pi Zero comes with a 40-pin **general purpose input/output** (**GPIO**) header that is arranged in two rows of 20 pins. The Raspberry Pi Zero's GPIO interface is shipped without a soldered header. The GPIO header is used to interface sensors, control actuators, and interface appliances. The GPIO header also consists of communication interfaces such as UART and I2C. We will discuss the GPIO in detail in the second chapter.

6. **RUN and TV pins**: There are two pins labeled as **RUN** below the GPIO header. These pins are used to reset the Raspberry Pi using a small tactile switch/push button. The **TV** pin is used to provide a composite video output.

7. **Camera interface**: Raspberry Pi Zero boards (version 1.3 or higher) come with a camera interface. This enables interfacing a camera designed by the Raspberry Pi Foundation (`https://www.raspberrypi.org/products/camera-module-v2/`).

All these features of the Raspberry Pi have enabled them to be used by hobbyists in projects involving home automation, holiday decorations, and more, limited only by your imagination. Scientists have used them in experiments, including tracking of bees, tracking wildlife, perform computation-intensive experiments. Engineers have used the Raspberry Pi to build robots, mine bitcoins, check Internet speeds to send Twitter messages when the speeds are slow, and order pizza!

# The setup of the Raspberry Pi Zero

In this section, we will solder some headers onto the Raspberry Pi, load the OS onto a micro SD card, and fire the Raspberry Pi Zero for the first example.

# Soldering the GPIO headers

In this book, we will discuss the different aspects of Python programming using the Raspberry Pi's GPIO pins. The Raspberry Pi Zero ships without the GPIO header pins. Let's go ahead and solder the GPIO pins. We have also uploaded a video tutorials to this book's website that demonstrates soldering the headers onto the Raspberry Pi Zero.

As mentioned before, the Raspberry Pi's GPIO section consists of 40 pins. This is arranged in two rows of 20 pins each. We will need either two sets of 20-pin male headers or a 20-pin double-row male header. These are available from vendors such as **Digikey** and **Mouser**. The headers for the Raspberry Pi are also sold as a kit by vendors like the Pi Hut (https://thepihut.com/collections/raspberry-pi-zero/products/raspberry-pi-zero-essential-kit).

2x20 headers for the Raspberry Pi Zero

In order to solder the headers onto the Raspberry Pi Zero, arrange the headers on a breadboard, as shown in the following figure:

Arranging the headers to solder onto the Raspberry Pi

Perform the following steps:

1. Arrange the Raspberry Pi on top of the headers upside down.
2. Gently hold the Raspberry Pi (to make sure that the headers are positioned correctly while soldering) and solder the headers onto the Raspberry Pi.

3. Inspect the board to ensure that the headers are soldered properly and carefully remove the Raspberry Pi Zero off the breadboard.

Headers soldered onto the Raspberry Pi

We are all set to make use of the GPIO pins in this book! Let's move on to the next section.

Soldering the headers onto the Raspberry Pi using a breadboard might damage the breadboard if the right temperature setting isn't used. The metal contacts of the breadboard might permanently expand resulting in permanent damage. Training in basic soldering techniques is crucial, and there are plenty of tutorials on this topic.

# Enclosure for the Raspberry Pi Zero

Setting up a Raspberry Pi zero inside an enclosure is completely optional but definitely useful while working on your projects. There are a plenty of enclosures sold by vendors. Alternatively, you may download an enclosure design from **Thingiverse** and 3D print them. We found this enclosure to suit our needs at
`http://www.thingiverse.com/thing:1203246` as it provides access to the GPIO headers. 3D printing services such as **3D Hubs** (`https://www.3dhubs.com/`) would print the enclosure for a charge of $9 via a local printer. Alternately, you can also use predesigned project enclosures or design one that can be constructed using **plexiglass** or similar materials.

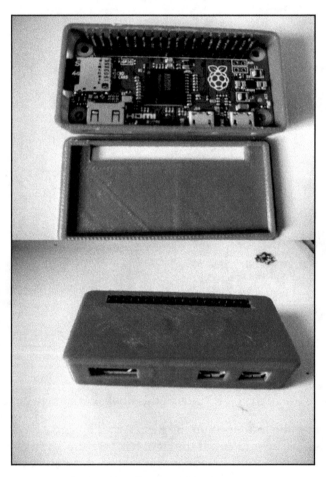

Raspberry Pi Zero in an enclosure

# OS setup for the Raspberry Pi

Let's go ahead and prepare a micro SD card to set up the Raspberry Pi Zero. In this book, we will be working with the **Raspbian OS**. The Raspbian OS has a wide user base, and the OS is officially supported by the Raspberry Pi Foundation. Hence, it is easier to find support on forums while working on projects as more people are familiar with the OS.

## micro SD card preparation

If you had purchased a micro SD card that comes pre-flashed with the Raspbian **New Out of the Box Software** (**NOOBS**) image, you may skip the micro SD card preparation:

1. The first step is downloading the Raspbian NOOBS image. The image can be downloaded from `https://www.raspberrypi.org/downloads/noobs/`.

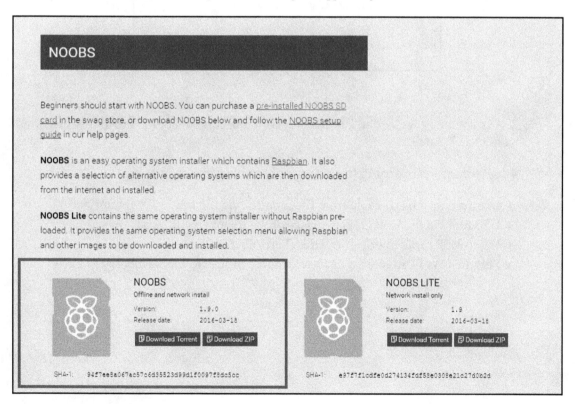

Downloads the Raspberry Pi NOOBS image

2. Format your SD card using the **SD Card Formatter** tool. Make sure that the **FORMAT SIZE ADJUSTMENT** is **ON** as shown in the snapshot (available from `https://www.sdcard.org/downloads/formatter_4/index.html`):

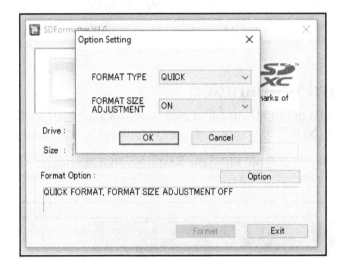

Format the SD card

3. Extract the downloaded ZIP file and copy the contents of the file to the formatted micro SD card.

4. Set up the Raspberry Pi (not necessarily in the same order):

   - Interface the HDMI cable from the monitor via the mini HDMI interface
   - USB hub via the USB OTG interface of the Raspberry Pi Zero
   - Micro-USB cable to power the Raspberry Pi Zero
   - Plug in a Wi-Fi adapter, a keyboard, and a mouse to the Raspberry Pi Zero

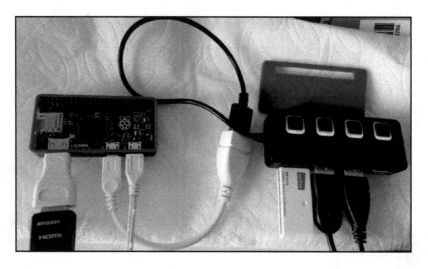

Raspberry Pi Zero with the keyboard, the mouse, and the Wi-Fi adapter

5. Power up the Raspberry Pi, and it should automatically flash the OS onto the SD card and launch the desktop at startup.

6. The first step after startup is changing the Raspberry Pi's password. Go to *menu* (the Raspberry Pi symbol located at the top-left corner) and select **Raspberry Pi Configuration** under **Preferences**.

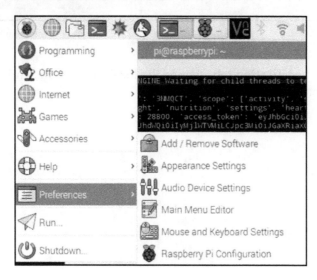

Launch Raspberry Pi configuration

7.  Under the System tab, change the password:

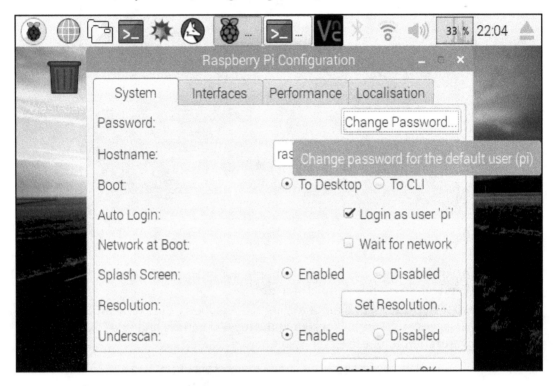

Change the password

8.  Under the **Localisation** tab, change the locale, time zone, and keyboard settings based upon your region.

9. When the installation is complete, connect the Raspberry Pi Zero to the wireless network (using the wireless tab on the top right).

Raspberry Pi desktop upon launch

10. Let's launch the command-line terminal of the Raspberry Pi to perform some software updates.

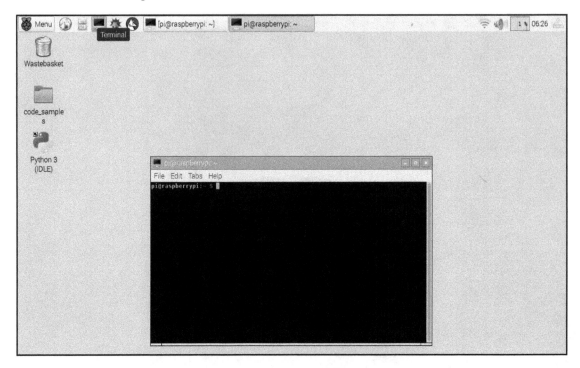

Launching the command-line terminal

11. Run the following commands from the command-line terminal:

```
sudo apt-get update
sudo apt-get upgrade
```

The OS upgrade should complete within a couple of minutes.

 The Raspberry Pi Foundation hosts a video on its website that provides a visual aid to set up the Raspberry Pi. This video is available at https://vimeo.com/90518800.

# Let's learn Python!

Python is a high-level programming language invented by Guido Van Rossum. It is advantageous to learn Python using the Raspberry Pi for the following reasons:

- It has a very simple syntax and hence is very easy to understand.
- It offers the flexibility of implementing ideas as a sequence of scripts. This is helpful to hobbyists to implement their ideas.
- There are Python libraries for the Raspberry Pi's GPIO. This enables easy interfacing of sensors/appliances with the Raspberry Pi.
- Python is used in a wide range of applications by technology giants such as Google. These applications range from simple robots to personal AI assistance and control modules in space.
- The Raspberry Pi has a growing fan base. This combined with the vast user base of Python means that there is no scarcity of learning resources or support for projects.

In this book, we will learn Python version 3.x. We will learn each major aspect of Python programming using a demonstrative example. Find out the awesomeness of Python by learning to do things by yourself! Keep in mind that there is Python 2.x, and it has subtle differences from Python 3.x.

 If you are comfortable with the Linux command-line terminal, we recommend setting up your Raspberry Pi for remote development, as shown in `Chapter 11`, *Tips and Tricks*.

# The Hello World example

Since we are done setting up the Raspberry Pi, let's get things rolling by writing our first piece of code in Python. While learning a new programming language, it is customary to get started by printing `Hello World` on the computer screen. Let's print the following message: `I am excited to learn Python programming with the Raspberry Pi Zero` using Python.

In this book, we will learn Python using the **Integrated Development and Learning Environment** (**IDLE**) tool. We chose IDLE for the following reasons:

- The tool is installed and shipped as a package in the Raspbian OS image. No additional installation is required.
- It is equipped with an interactive tool that enables performing checks on a piece of code or a specific feature of the Python language.
- It comes with a text editor that enables writing code according to the conventions of the Python programming language. The text editor provides a color code for different elements of a Python script. This helps in writing a Python script with relative ease.
- The tool enables a step-by-step execution of any code sample and identify problems in it.

# Setting up your Raspberry Pi Zero for Python programming

Before we get started, let's go ahead and set up the Raspberry Pi Zero to suit our needs:

1. Let's add a shortcut to IDLE3 (for developing in Python 3.x) on the Raspberry Pi's desktop. Under the Programming submenu (located at the top-left corner of your Raspberry Pi Zero's desktop), right-click on **Python 3 (IDLE)** and click on **Add to desktop**. This adds a shortcut to the IDLE tool on your desktop thus making it easily accessible.

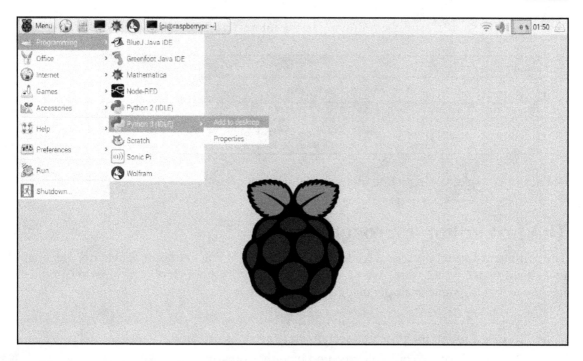

Add shortcut to IDLE3 to the Raspberry Pi's desktop

2.  In order to save all the code samples, let's go ahead and create a folder named code_samples on the Raspberry Pi's desktop. Right-click on your desktop and create a new folder.

## IDLE's interactive tool

Let's write our first example using IDLE's interactive tool:

1.  Launch the IDLE3 (meant for Python 3.x) tool from the Raspberry Pi Zero's desktop by double-clicking on it.
2.  From the IDLE's interactive command-line tool, type the following line:

```
print("I am excited to learn Python with the Raspberry Pi Zero")
```

3. This should print the following to the interactive command-line tool's screen:

```
Python 3.4.2 Shell                                          _  □  ✕

File  Edit  Shell  Debug  Options  Windows  Help

Python 3.4.2 (default, Oct 19 2014, 13:31:11)
[GCC 4.9.1] on linux
Type "copyright", "credits" or "license()" for more information.
>>> print("I am excited to learn Python with the Raspberry Pi Zero")
```

We did it! We wrote a single line that prints out a line of text to the Raspberry Pi's screen.

# The text editor approach

The command-line tool is useful for test coding logic, but it is neither practical nor elegant to write code using the interactive tool. It is easier to write a bunch of code at a time and test it. Let's repeat the same example using IDLE's text editor:

1. Launch IDLE's text editor (in IDLE, **File | New File**), enter the hello world line discussed in the previous section and save it as helloworld.py.

2. Now, the code could be executed by either pressing the *F5* key or clicking on **Run Module** from the drop-down menu **Run**, and you will get the output as shown in the following figure:

```
>>> ============================= RESTART =============================
>>>
I am excited to learn Python with the Raspberry Pi Zero
>>> |
```

# Launching the Python interpreter via the Linux Terminal

It is also possible to use the Python interpreter via the **Linux Terminal**. Programmers mostly use this to test their code or refer to the Python documentation tool, **pydoc**. This approach is convenient if the readers plan to use a text editor other than IDLE:

1.  Launch the Raspberry Pi's command-line terminal from the desktop toolbar.

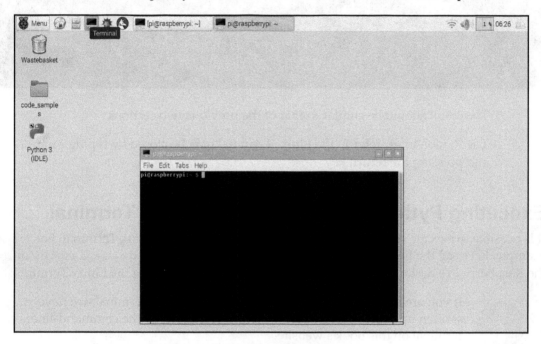

Launching the command-line terminal

2.  Type the command,python3 and press *Enter*. This should launch Python 3.x on the terminal.
3.  Now, try running the same piece of code discussed in the previous section:

```
print("I am excited to learn Python with the Raspberry Pi Zero")
```

This would give the following screenshot as the result:

```
                              pi@raspberrypi: ~
File  Edit  Tabs  Help
pi@raspberrypi:~ $ python3
Python 3.4.2 (default, Oct 19 2014, 13:31:11)
[GCC 4.9.1] on linux
Type "help", "copyright", "credits" or "license" for more information.
>>> print("I am excited to learn Python with the Raspberry Pi Zero")
I am excited to learn Python with the Raspberry Pi Zero
>>>
```

The result should be similar to that of the previous two sections

The Python interpreter in the Linux Terminal may be closed by typing `exit()` and pressing the return key

# Executing Python scripts using the Linux Terminal

It is possible to execute code written using any text editor via the Linux Terminal. For example, Let's say the file `helloworld.py` is saved in a folder named `code_samples` on the Raspberry Pi's desktop. This file may be executed as follows from the Linux Terminal:

 If you are not familiar with the Linux command-line terminal, we have written up some tutorials to familiarize yourself with the command-line terminal on this book's website.

1. On the Linux Terminal, switch to the directory where the Python script is located:

   **cd /home/pi/Desktop/code_samples**

2. Execute the Python script as follows:

   **python3 helloworld.py**

3. Alternatively, the Python script could be executed using its absolute location path:

   **python3 /home/pi/Desktop/code_samples/hello_world.py**

We did it! We just wrote our first piece of code and discussed different ways to execute the code.

# The print() function

In our first `helloworld` example, we discussed printing something on the screen. We used the `print()` function to obtain our result. In Python, a **function** is a code block that executes a set of defined tasks. The `print()` function is a part of Python's standard library that prints any combination of alphanumeric characters that is passed as an argument between the quotes. The `print()` function is used to print information to the screen. It is especially helpful while trying to debug the code. In this example, the `print()` function was used to print a message on the screen.

In this chapter, the function `print()` executed the string `I am excited to learn Python programming with the Raspberry Pi Zero` (we will discuss strings in the later section of this book). It is also possible to write custom function to execute a repetitive task required by the user.

Similarly, the `exit()` function executes the predefined task of exiting the Python interpreter at the user's call.

# The help() function

While getting started, it is going to be difficult to remember the syntax of every function in Python. It is possible to refer to a function's documentation and syntax using the help function in Python. For example, in order to find the use of the print function in Python, we can call help on the command-line terminal or the interactive shell as follows:

```
help(print)
```

This would return a detailed description of the function and its syntax:

```
>>> help(print)
Help on built-in function print in module builtins:

print(...)
    print(value, ..., sep=' ', end='\n', file=sys.stdout, flush=False)

    Prints the values to a stream, or to sys.stdout by default.
    Optional keyword arguments:
    file:  a file-like object (stream); defaults to the current sys.stdout.
    sep:   string inserted between values, default a space.
    end:   string appended after the last value, default a newline.
    flush: whether to forcibly flush the stream.
```

# Summary

That's it! In this chapter, we set up the Raspberry Pi Zero to write our first program in Python. We also explored different options to write a Python program. You are now ready and on your way to learn Python with the Raspberry Pi. In the next chapter, we will dig deeper and learn more about the GPIO pins while executing a simple project that makes LEDs blink.

# 2

# Arithmetic Operations, Loops, and Blinky Lights

In the previous chapter, we discussed printing a line of text on the screen. In this chapter, we will review arithmetic operations and variables in Python. We will also discuss strings and accepting user inputs in Python. You will learn about the Raspberry Pi's GPIO and its features and write code in Python that makes an LED blink using the Raspberry Pi's GPIO. We will also discuss a practical application of controlling the Raspberry Pi's GPIO.

In this chapter, we will cover the following topics:

- Arithmetic operations in Python
- Bitwise operators in Python
- Logical operators in Python
- Data types and variables in Python
- Loops in Python
- Raspberry Pi Zero's GPIO interface.

## Hardware required for this chapter

In this chapter, we will be discussing examples where we will be controlling the Raspberry Pi's GPIO. We will need a breadboard, jumper wires, LEDs, and some resistors (330 or 470 Ohms) to discuss these examples.

We will also need some optional hardware that we will discuss in the last section of this chapter.

# Arithmetic operations

Python enables performing all the standard arithmetic operations. Let's launch the Python interpreter and learn more:

- **Addition**: Two numbers can be added using the + operand. The result is printed on the screen. Try the following example using the python interpreter:

  ```
  >>>123+456
  579
  ```

- **Subtraction**: Two numbers can be added using the – operand:

  ```
  >>>456-123
  333
  >>>123-456
  -333
  ```

- **Multiplication**: Two numbers can be multiplied as follows:

  ```
  >>>123*456
  56088
  ```

- **Division**: Two numbers can be divided as follows:

  ```
  >>>456/22
  20.727272727272727
  >>>456/2.0
  228.0
  >>>int(456/228)
  2
  ```

- **Modulus operator**: In Python, the modulus operator (%) returns the remainder of a division operation:

  ```
  >>>4%2
  0
  >>>3%2
  1
  ```

- The **floor operator** (//) is the opposite of the modulus operator. This operator returns the floor of the quotient, that is, the integer result, and discards the fractions:

  ```
  >>>9//7
  1
  ```

```
>>>7//3
2
>>>79//25
3
```

# Bitwise operators in Python

In Python, it is possible to perform bit-level operations on numbers. This is especially helpful while parsing information from certain sensors. For example, Some sensors share their output at a certain frequency. When a new data point is available, a certain bit is set indicating that the data is available. Bitwise operators can be used to check whether a particular bit is set before retrieving the datapoint from the sensor.

If you are interested in a deep dive on bitwise operators, we recommend getting started at `https://en.wikipedia.org/wiki/Bitwise_operation`.

Consider the numbers 3 and 2 whose binary equivalents are 011 and 010, respectively. Let's take a look at different operators that perform the operation on every bit of the number:

- **The AND operator**: The AND operator is used to perform the AND operation on two numbers. Try this using the Python interpreter:

  ```
  >>>3&2
  2
  ```

  This is equivalent to the following AND operation:

  ```
  0 1 1 &
  0 1 0
  --------
  0 1 0 (the binary representation of the number 2)
  ```

- **The OR operator**: The OR operator is used to perform the OR operation on two numbers as follows:

  ```
  >>>3|2
  3
  ```

  This is equivalent to the following OR operation:

  ```
  0 1 1 OR
  0 1 0
  --------
  0 1 1 (the binary representation of the number 3)
  ```

- **The NOT operator**: The NOT operator flips the bits of a number. see the following example:

```
>>>~1
-2
```

In the preceding example, the bits are flipped, that is, 1 as 0 and 0 as 1. So, the binary representation of 1 is 0001 and when the bitwise NOT operation is performed, the result is 1110. The interpreter returns the result as -2 because negative numbers are stored as their *two's complement*. The two's complement of 1 is -2.

 For a better understanding of two's complement and so on, we recommend reading the following articles, https://wiki.python.org/moin/BitwiseOperators and https://en.wikipedia.org/wiki/Two's_complement.

- **The XOR operator**: An exclusive OR operation can be performed as follows:

```
>>>3^2
1
```

- **Left shift operator**: The left shift operator enables shifting the bits of a given value to the left by the desired number of places. For example, bit shifting the number 3 to the left gives us the number 6. The binary representation of the number 3 is 0011. Left shifting the bits by one position will give us 0110, that is, the number 6:

```
>>>3<<1
6
```

- **Right shift operator**: The right shift operator enables shifting the bits of a given value to the right by the desired number of places. Launch the command-line interpreter and try this yourself. What happens when you bit shift the number 6 to the right by one position?

# Logical operators

**Logical operators** are used to check different conditions and execute the code accordingly. For example, detecting a button interfaced to the Raspberry Pi's GPIO being pressed and executing a specific task as a consequence. Let's discuss the basic logical operators:

- **EQUAL**: The EQUAL (==) operator is used to compare if two values are equal:

  ```
  >>>3==3
  True
  >>>3==2
  False
  ```

- **NOT EQUAL**: The NOT EQUAL (!=) operator compares two values and returns True if they are not equal:

  ```
  >>>3!=2
  True
  >>>2!=2
  False
  ```

- **GREATER THAN**: This operator (>) returns True if one value is greater than the other value:

  ```
  >>>3>2
  True
  >>>2>3
  False
  ```

- **LESS THAN**: This operator compares two values and returns True if one value is smaller than the other:

  ```
  >>>2<3
  True
  >>>3<2
  False
  ```

- **GREATER THAN OR EQUAL TO (>=)**: This operator compares two values and returns True if one value is greater/bigger than or equal to the other value:

  ```
  >>>4>=3
  True
  >>>3>=3
  True
  >>>2>=3
  False
  ```

- **LESS THAN OR EQUAL TO (<=)**: This operator compares two values and returns `True` if one value is smaller than or equal to the other value:

```
>>>2<=2
True
>>>2<=3
True
>>>3<=2
False
```

# Data types and variables in Python

In Python, **variables** are used to store a result or a value in the computer's memory during the execution of a program. Variables enable easy access to a specific location on the computer's memory and enables writing user-readable code.

For example, let's consider a scenario where a person wants a new ID card from an office or a university. The person would be asked to fill out an application form with relevant information, including their name, department, and emergency contact information. The form would have the requisite fields. This would enable the office manager to refer to the form while creating a new ID card.

Similarly, variables simplify code development by providing means to store information in the computer's memory. It would be very difficult to write code if one had to write code keeping the storage memory map in mind. For example, it is easier to use the variable called name rather than a specific memory address like `0x3745092`.

There are different kinds of data types in Python. Let's review the different data types:

- In general, names, street addresses, and so on are a combination of alphanumeric characters. In Python, they are stored as *strings*. Strings in Python are represented and stored in variables as follows:

```
>>>name = 'John Smith'
>>>address = '123 Main Street'
```

- *Numbers* in Python could be stored as follows:

```
>>>age = 29
>>>employee_id = 123456
>>>height = 179.5
>>>zip_code = 94560
```

- Python also enables storing *boolean* variables. For example, a person's organ donor status can be either as `True` or `False`:

  ```
  >>>organ_donor = True
  ```

- It is possible to *assign* values to multiple variables at the same time:

  ```
  >>>a = c= 1
  >>>b = a
  ```

- A variable may be *deleted* as follows:

  ```
  >>>del(a)
  ```

There are other data types in Python, including lists, tuples, and dictionaries. We will discuss this in detail in the next chapter.

# Reading inputs from the user

In the previous chapter, we printed something on the screen for the user. Now, we will discuss a simple program where we ask the user to enter two numbers and the program returns the sum of two numbers. For now, we are going to pretend that the user always provides a valid input.

In Python, user input to a Python program can be provided using the `input()` function (`https://docs.python.org/3/library/functions.html#input`):

```
var = input("Enter the first number: ")
```

In the preceding example, we are making use of the `input()` function to seek the user's input of the number. The `input()` function takes the prompt (`"Enter the first number: "`) as an argument and returns the user input. In this example, the user input is stored in the variable, `var`. In order to add two numbers, we make use of the `input()` function to request user to provide two numbers as input:

```
var1 = input("Enter the first number: ")
var2 = input("Enter the second number: ")
total = int(var1) + int(var2)
print("The sum is %d" % total)
```

We are making use of the `input()` function to seek user input on two numbers. In this case, the user number is stored in `var1` and `var2`, respectively.

The user input is a string. We need to convert them into integers before adding them. We can convert a string to an integer using the `int()` function (`https://docs.python.org/3/library/functions.html#int`).

The `int()` function takes the string as an argument and returns the converted integer. The converted integers are added and stored in the variable, `total`. The preceding example is available for download along with this chapter as `input_function.py`.

 If the user input is invalid, the `int()` function will throw an exception indicating that an error has occurred. Hence, we assumed that user inputs are valid in this example. In a later chapter, we will discuss catching exceptions that are caused by invalid inputs.

The following snapshot shows the program output:

```
pi@raspberrypi: ~/Documents/pywpi/chapter_2
File  Edit  Tabs  Help
pi@raspberrypi:~/Documents/pywpi/chapter_2 $ python3 input_function.py
Enter the first number: 3
Enter the second number: 2
The sum is 5
```

The input_function.py output

# The formatted string output

Let's revisit the example discussed in the previous section. We printed the result as follows:

```python
print("The sum is %d" % total)
```

In Python, it is possible to format a string to display the result. In the earlier example, we make use of `%d` to indicate that it is a placeholder for an integer variable. This enables printing the string with the integer. Along with the string that is passed an argument to the `print()` function, the variable that needs to be printed is also passed an argument. In the earlier example, the variables are passed using the `%` operator. It is also possible to pass multiple variables:

```python
print("The sum of %d and %d is %d" % (var1, var2, total))
```

It is also possible to format a string as follows:

```
print("The sum of 3 and 2 is {total}".format(total=5))
```

# The str.format() method

The `format()` method enables formatting the string using braces ({ }) as placeholders. In the preceding example, we use `total` as a placeholder and use the format method of the string class to fill each place holder.

# An exercise for the reader

Make use of the `format()` method to format a string with more than one variable.

Let's build a console/command-line application that takes inputs from the user and print it on the screen. Let's create a new file named `input_test.py`, (available along with this chapter's downloads) take some user inputs and print them on the screen:

```
name = input("What is your name? ")
address = input("What is your address? ")
age = input("How old are you? ")

print("My name is " + name)
print("I am " + age + " years old")
print("My address is " + address)
```

Execute the program and see what happens:

```
pi@raspberrypi:~/Documents/pywpi/chapter_2 $ python3 input_test.py
What is your name? Sai
What is your address? 123 Main Street, Newark, CA
How old are you? 29
My name is Sai
I am 29 years old
My address is 123 Main Street, Newark, CA
```

The input_test.py output

The preceding example is available for download along with this chapter as `input_test.py`.

## Another exercise for the reader

Repeat the earlier example using the string formatting techniques.

# Concatenating strings

In the preceding example, we printed the user inputs in combination with another string. For example, we took the user input `name` and printed the sentence as `My name is Sai`. The process of appending one string to another is called **concatenation**.

In Python, strings can be concatenated by adding + between two strings:

```
name = input("What is your name? ")
print("My name is " + name)
```

It is possible to concatenate two strings, but it is not possible to concatenate an integer. Let's consider the following example:

```
id = 5
print("My id is " + id)
```

It would throw an error implying that integers and strings cannot be combined:

```
Traceback (most recent call last):
  File "<stdin>", line 1, in <module>
TypeError: Can't convert 'int' object to str implicitly
```

An exception

It is possible to convert an integer to string and concatenate it to another string:

```
print("My id is " + str(id))
```

This would give the following result:

```
>>> print("My id is " + str(id))
My id is 5
```

# Loops in Python

Sometimes, a specific task has to be repeated several times. In such cases, we could use **loops**. In Python, there are two types of loops, namely the `for` loop and `while` loop. Let's review them with specific examples.

# A for loop

In Python, a `for` loop is used to execute a task for *n* times. A for loop iterates through each element of a sequence. This sequence could be a dictionary, list, or any other iterator. For example, let's discuss an example where we execute a loop:

```
for i in range(0, 10):
    print("Loop execution no: ", i)
```

In the preceding example, the `print` statement is executed 10 times:

```
Loop execution no: 0
Loop execution no: 1
Loop execution no: 2
Loop execution no: 3
Loop execution no: 4
Loop execution no: 5
Loop execution no: 6
Loop execution no: 7
Loop execution no: 8
Loop execution no: 9
```

In order to execute the `print` task 10 times, the `range()` function (https://docs.python.org/2/library/functions.html#range) was used. The `range` function generates a list of numbers for a start and stop values that are passed as an arguments to the function. In this case, 0 and 10 are passed as arguments to the `range()` function. This returns a list containing numbers from 0 to 9. The `for` loop iterates through the code block for each element in steps of 1. The `range` function can also generate a list of numbers in steps of 2. This is done by passing the start value, stop value, and the step value as arguments to the `range()` function:

```
for i in range(0, 20, 2):
    print("Loop execution no: ", i)
```

In this example, 0 is the start value, 20 is the stop value, and 2 is the step value. This generates a list of 10 numbers in steps of two:

```
Loop execution no: 0
Loop execution no: 2
Loop execution no: 4
Loop execution no: 6
Loop execution no: 8
Loop execution no: 10
Loop execution no: 12
Loop execution no: 14
Loop execution no: 16
Loop_execution no: 18
```

The range function can be used to count down from a given number. Let's say we would like to count down from 10 to 1:

```
for i in range(10, 0, -1):
    print("Count down no: ", i)
```

The output would be something like:

```
Count down no:   10
Count down no:   9
Count down no:   8
Count down no:   7
Count down no:   6
Count down no:   5
Count down no:   4
Count down no:   3
Count down no:   2
Count down no:   1
```

The general syntax of the range function is range(start, stop, step_count). It generates a sequence of numbers from start to n-1 where n is the stop value.

# Indentation

Note the *indentation* in the `for` loop block:

```
for i in range(10, 1, -1):
    print("Count down no: ", i)
```

Python executes the block of code under the `for` loop statement. It is one of the features of the Python programming language. It executes any piece of code under the `for` loop as long as it has same level of indentation:

```
for i in range(0,10):
    #start of block
    print("Hello")
    #end of block
```

The indentation has the following two uses:

- It makes the code readable
- It helps us identify the block of code to be executed in a loop

It is important to pay attention to indentation in Python as it directly affects how a piece of code is executed.

## Nested loops

In Python, it is possible to implement *a loop within a loop*. For example, let's say we have to print x and y coordinates of a map. We can use nested loops to implement this:

```
for x in range(0,3):
    for y in range(0,3):
        print(x,y)
```

The expected output is:

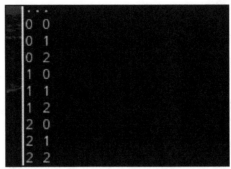

Be careful about code indentation in nested loops as it may throw errors. Consider the following example:

```
for x in range(0,10):
    for y in range(0,10):
    print(x,y)
```

The Python interpreter would throw the following error:

```
SyntaxError: expected an indented block
```

This is visible in the following screenshot:

```
>>> for x in range(0, 10):
...         for y in range(0, 10):
...         print(x,y)
  File "<stdin>", line 3
    print(x,y)
             ^
IndentationError: expected an indented block
```

Hence, it is important to pay attention to indentation in Python (especially nested loops) to successfully execute the code. IDLE's text editor automatically indents code as you write them. This should aid with understanding indentation in Python.

# A while loop

`while` loops are used when a specific task is supposed to be executed until a specific condition is met. `while` loops are commonly used to execute code in an infinite loop. Let's look at a specific example where we would like to print the value of i from 0 to 9:

```
i=0
while i<10:
    print("The value of i is ",i)
    i+=1
```

Inside the `while` loop, we increment i by 1 for every iteration. The value of i is incremented as follows:

```
i += 1
```

This is equivalent to i = i+1.

This example would execute the code until the value of i is less than 10. It is also possible to execute something in an infinite loop:

```
i=0
while True:
    print("The value of i is ",i)
    i+=1
```

The execution of this infinite loop can be stopped by pressing *Ctrl* + *C* on your keyboard.

It is also possible to have nested `while` loops:

```
i=0
j=0
while i<10:
    while j<10:
        print("The value of i,j is ",i,",",j)
        i+=1
        j+=1
```

Similar to `for` loops, `while` loops also rely on the indented code block to execute a piece of code.

Python enables printing a combination of strings and integers as long as they are presented as arguments to the `print` function separated by commas. In the earlier-mentioned example, `The value of i,j is,i` are arguments to the `print` function. You will learn more about functions and arguments in the next chapter. This feature enables formatting the output string to suit our needs.

# Raspberry Pi's GPIO

The Raspberry Pi Zero comes with a 40-pin GPIO header. Out of these 40 pins, we can use 26 pins either to read inputs (from sensors) or control outputs. The other pins are power supply pins (**5V**, **3.3V**, and **Ground** pins):

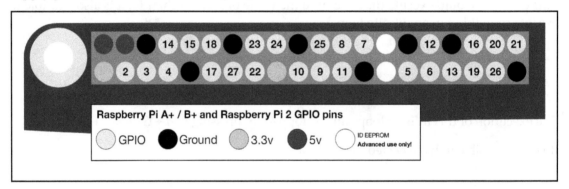

Raspberry Pi Zero GPIO mapping (source: https://www.raspberrypi.org/documentation/usage/gpio-plus-and-raspi2/README.md)

We can use up to 26 pins of the Raspberry Pi's GPIO to interface appliances and control them. But, there are certain pins that have an alternative function, which will be discussed in the later chapters.

The earlier image shows the mapping of the Raspberry Pi's GPIO pins. The numbers in the circle correspond to the pin numbers on the Raspberry Pi's processor. For example, GPIO pin **2** (second pin from the left on the bottom row) corresponds to the GPIO pin **2** on the Raspberry Pi's processor and not the physical pin location on the GPIO header.

In the beginning, it might be confusing to try and understand the pin mapping. Keep a GPIO pin handout (available for download along with this chapter) for your reference. It takes some time to get used to the GPIO pin mapping of the Raspberry Pi Zero.

 The Raspberry Pi Zero's GPIO pins are 3.3V tolerant, that is, if a voltage greater than 3.3V is applied to the pin, it may permanently damage the pin. When set to *high*, the pins are set to 3.3V and 0V when the pins are set to low.

# Blinky lights

Let's discuss an example where we make use of the Raspberry Pi Zero's GPIO. We will interface an LED to the Raspberry Pi Zero and make it blink *on* and *off* with a 1-second interval.

Let's wire up the Raspberry Pi zero to get started:

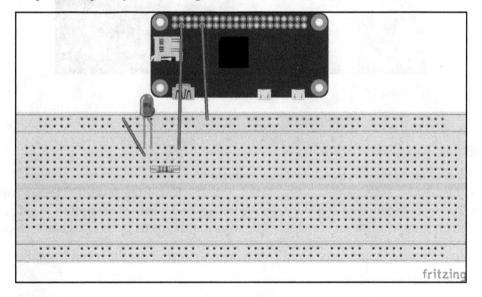

Blinky schematic generated using Fritzing

In the preceding schematic, the GPIO pin 2 is connected to the anode (the longest leg) of the LED. The cathode of the LED is connected to the ground pin of the Raspberry Pi Zero. A 330 Ohm current limiting resistor is also used to limit the flow of the current.

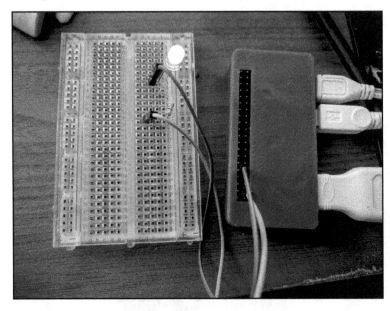

Breadboard connections to the Raspberry Pi Zero

# Code

We will make use of the `python3-gpiozero` library (`https://gpiozero.readthedocs.io/en/v1.3.1/`). The **Raspbian Jessie** OS image comes with the pre-installed library. It is very simple to use, and it is the best option to get started as a beginner. It supports a standard set of devices that helps us get started easily.

For example, in order to interface an LED, we need to import the `LED` class from the `gpiozero` library:

```
from gpiozero import LED
```

We will be turning the LED *on* and *off* at a 1-second interval. In order to do so, we will be *importing* the `time` library. In Python, we need to import a library to make use of it. Since we interfaced the LED to the GPIO pin 2, let's make a mention of that in our code:

```
import time

led = LED(2)
```

We just created a variable named `led` and defined that we will be making use of GPIO pin 2 in the `LED` class. Let's make use of a `while` loop to turn the LED on and off with a 1-second interval.

The `gpiozero` library's LED class comes with functions named `on()` and `off()` to set the GPIO pin 2 to high and low, respectively:

```
while True:
    led.on()
    time.sleep(1)
    led.off()
    time.sleep(1)
```

In Python's time library, there is a `sleep` function that enables introducing a 1-second delay between turning on/off the LED. This is executed in an infinite loop! We just built a practical example using the Raspberry Pi Zero.

Putting all the code together in a file named `blinky.py` (available for download along with this book), run the code from the command-line terminal (alternatively, you may use IDLE3):

```
python3 blinky.py
```

# The applications of GPIO control

Now that we have implemented our first example, let's discuss some possible applications of being able to control the GPIO. We could use the Raspberry Pi's GPIO to control the lights in our homes. We will make use of the same example to control a table lamp!

There is a product called the **PowerSwitch Tail II** (http://www.powerswitchtail.com/Pages/default.aspx) that enables interfacing AC appliances like a table lamp to a Raspberry Pi. The PowerSwitch Tail comes with control pins (that can take a 3.3V high signal) that could be used to turn on/off a lamp. The switch comes with the requisite circuitry/protection to interface it directly to a Raspberry Pi Zero:

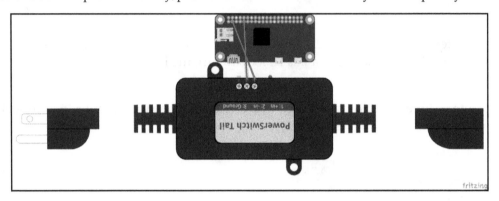

The Pi Zero interfaced to the PowerSwitch Tail II

Let's take the same example from the previous section and connect the GPIO pin 2 to the **+in** pin of the PowerSwitch Tail. Let's connect the ground pin of the Raspberry Pi Zero's GPIO header to the PowerSwitch Tail's **-in** pain. The PowerSwitch Tail should be connected to the AC mains. The lamp should be connected to the AC output of the switch. If we use the same piece of code and connect a lamp to the PowerSwitch Tail, we should be able to turn on/off with a 1-second interval.

PowerSwitch Tail II connected to a Raspberry Pi Zero

This appliance control using the LED blinking code is just an example. It is not recommended to turn on/off a table lamp at such short intervals. In future chapters, we will make use of the Raspberry Pi Zero's GPIO to control appliances from anywhere on the Internet.

# Summary

In this chapter, we reviewed the integers, boolean, and string data types as well as arithmetic operations and logical operators in Python. We also discussed accepting user inputs and loops. We introduced ourselves to the Raspberry Pi Zero's GPIO and discussed an LED blinking example. We took the same example to control a table lamp!

Have you heard of the chat application named *Slack*? How about controlling a table lamp at home from your laptop at work? If that piques your interest, work with us toward that over the next few chapters.

# 3
# Conditional Statements, Functions, and Lists

In this chapter, we will build upon what you learned in the previous chapter. You will learn about conditional statements and how to make use of logical operators to check conditions using conditional statements. Next, you will learn to write simple functions in Python and discuss interfacing inputs to the Raspberry Pi's GPIO header using a tactile switch (momentary push button). We will also discuss motor control (this is a run-up to the final project) using the Raspberry Pi Zero and control the motors using the switch inputs. Let's get to it!

In this chapter, we will discuss the following topics:

- Conditional statements in Python
    - Using conditional inputs to take actions based on GPIO pin states
    - Breaking out of loops using conditional statement
- Functions in Python
    - GPIO callback functions
- Motor control in Python

# Conditional statements

In Python, conditional statements are used to determine if a specific condition is met by testing whether a condition is true or false. Conditional statements are used to determine how a program is executed. For example, conditional statements could be used to determine whether it is time to turn on the lights. The syntax is as follows:

```
if condition_is_true:

    do_something()
```

The condition is usually tested using a logical operator, and the set of tasks under the indented block is executed. Let's consider the example, `check_address_if_statement.py` (available for download with this chapter) where the user input to a program needs to be verified using a yes or no question:

```
check_address = input("Is your address correct(yes/no)? ")
if check_address == "yes":
  print("Thanks. Your address has been saved")
if check_address == "no":
  del(address)
  print("Your address has been deleted. Try again")
```

In this example, the program expects a yes or no input. If the user provides the input yes, the condition if check_address == "yes" is true, the message Your address has been saved is printed on the screen.

Likewise, if the user input is no, the program executes the indented code block under the logical test condition if check_address == "no" and deletes the variable address.

# An if-else statement

In the preceding example, we used an if statement to test each condition. In Python, there is an alternative option named the if-else statement. The if-else statement enables testing an alternative condition if the main condition is not true:

```
check_address = input("Is your address correct(yes/no)? ")
if check_address == "yes":
  print("Thanks. Your address has been saved")
else:
  del(address)
  print("Your address has been deleted. Try again")
```

In this example, if the user input is yes, the indented code block under if is executed. Otherwise, the code block under else is executed.

# if-elif-else statement

In the preceding example, the program executes any piece of code under the else block for any user input other than yes that is if the user pressed the return key without providing any input or provided random characters instead of no, the if-elif-else statement works as follows:

```
check_address = input("Is your address correct(yes/no)? ")
if check_address == "yes":
    print("Thanks. Your address has been saved")
elif check_address == "no":
    del(address)
    print("Your address has been deleted. Try again")
else:
    print("Invalid input. Try again")
```

If the user input is yes, the indented code block under the if statement is executed. If the user input is no, the indented code block under elif (*else-if*) is executed. If the user input is something else, the program prints the message: Invalid input. Try again.

It is important to note that the code block indentation determines the block of code that needs to be executed when a specific condition is met. We recommend modifying the indentation of the conditional statement block and find out what happens to the program execution. This will help understand the importance of indentation in Python.

In the three examples that we discussed so far, it could be noted that an if statement does not need to be complemented by an else statement. The else and elif statements need to have a preceding if statement or the program execution would result in an error.

# Breaking out of loops

Conditional statements can be used to break out of a loop execution (`for` loop and `while` loop). When a specific condition is met, an `if` statement can be used to break out of a loop:

```
i = 0
while True:
  print("The value of i is ", i)
  i += 1
  if i > 100:
    break
```

In the preceding example, the `while` loop is executed in an infinite loop. The value of `i` is incremented and printed on the screen. The program breaks out of the `while` loop when the value of `i` is greater than `100` and the value of `i` is printed from 1 to 100.

# The applications of conditional statements: executing tasks using GPIO

In the previous chapter, we discussed interfacing outputs to the Raspberry Pi's GPIO. Let's discuss an example where a simple push button is pressed. A button press is detected by reading the GPIO pin state. We are going to make use of conditional statements to execute a task based on the GPIO pin state.

Let us connect a button to the Raspberry Pi's GPIO. All you need to get started are a button, pull-up resistor, and a few jumper wires. The figure given later shows an illustration on connecting the push button to the Raspberry Pi Zero. One of the push button's terminals is connected to the ground pin of the Raspberry Pi Zero's GPIO pin.

The schematic of the button's interface is shown here:

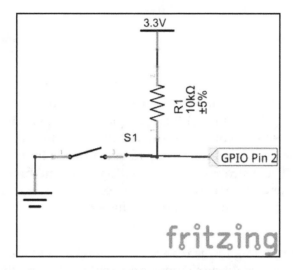

Raspberry Pi GPIO schematic

The other terminal of the push button is pulled up to 3.3V using a 10 K resistor. The junction of the push button terminal and the 10 K resistor is connected to the GPIO pin 2 (refer to the BCM GPIO pin map shared in the earlier chapter).

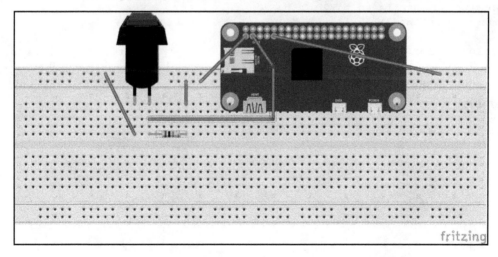

Interfacing the push button to the Raspberry Pi Zero's GPIO - an image generated using Fritzing

Let's review the code required to review the button state. We make use of loops and conditional statements to read the button inputs using the Raspberry Pi Zero.

We will be making use of the `gpiozero` library introduced in the previous chapter. The code sample for this section is `GPIO_button_test.py` and available for download along with this chapter.

In a later chapter, we will discuss **object-oriented programming (OOP)**. For now, let's briefly discuss the concept of classes for this example. A **class** in Python is a blueprint that contains all the attributes that define an object. For example, the `Button` class of the `gpiozero` library contains all attributes required to interface a button to the Raspberry Pi Zero's GPIO interface. These attributes include button states and functions required to check the button states and so on. In order to interface a button and read its states, we need to make use of this blueprint. The process of creating a copy of this blueprint is called instantiation.

Let's get started with importing the `gpiozero` library and instantiate the `Button` class of the `gpiozero` library (we will discuss Python's classes, objects, and their attributes in a later chapter). The button is interfaced to GPIO pin 2. We need to pass the pin number as an argument during instantiation:

```
from gpiozero import Button

#button is interfaced to GPIO 2
button = Button(2)
```

The `gpiozero` library's documentation is available at `http://gpiozero.readthedocs.io /en/v1.2.0/api_input.html`. According to the documentation, there is a variable named `is_pressed` in the `Button` class that could be tested using a conditional statement to determine if the button is pressed:

```
if button.is_pressed:
    print("Button pressed")
```

Whenever the button is pressed, the message `Button pressed` is printed on the screen. Let's stick this code snippet inside an infinite loop:

```
from gpiozero import Button

#button is interfaced to GPIO 2
button = Button(2)

while True:
   if button.is_pressed:
      print("Button pressed")
```

In an infinite `while` loop, the program constantly checks for a button press and prints the message as long as the button is being pressed. Once the button is released, it goes back to checking whether the button is pressed.

## Breaking out a loop by counting button presses

Let's review another example where we would like to count the number of button presses and break out of the infinite loop when the button has received a predetermined number of presses:

```
i = 0
while True:
   if button.is_pressed:
      button.wait_for_release()
      i += 1
      print("Button pressed")

   if i >= 10:
      break
```

The preceding example is available for downloading along with this chapter as `GPIO_button_loop_break.py`.

In this example, the program checks for the state of the `is_pressed` variable. On receiving a button press, the program can be paused until the button is released using the `wait_for_release` method. When the button is released, the variable used to store the number of presses is incremented by one.

The program breaks out of the infinite loop, when the button has received 10 presses.

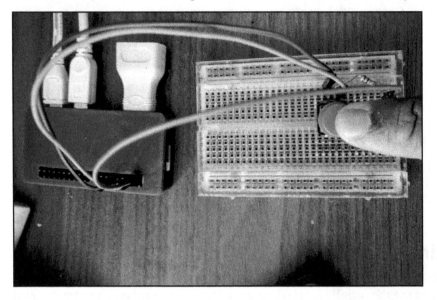

A red momentary push button interfaced to Raspberry Pi Zero GPIO pin 2

# Functions in Python

We briefly discussed functions in Python. Functions execute a predefined set of task. `print` is one example of a function in Python. It enables printing something to the screen. Let's discuss writing our own functions in Python.

A function can be declared in Python using the `def` keyword. A function could be defined as follows:

```
def my_func():
    print("This is a simple function")
```

In this function `my_func`, the `print` statement is written under an indented code block. Any block of code that is indented under the function definition is executed when the function is called during the code execution. The function could be executed as `my_func()`.

# Passing arguments to a function:

A function is always defined with parentheses. The parentheses are used to pass any requisite arguments to a function. Arguments are parameters required to execute a function. In the earlier example, there are no arguments passed to the function.

Let's review an example where we pass an argument to a function:

```
def add_function(a, b):
    c = a + b
    print("The sum of a and b is ", c)
```

In this example, a and b are arguments to the function. The function adds a and b and prints the sum on the screen. When the function add_function is called by passing the arguments 3 and 2 as add_function(3,2) where a is 3 and b is 2, respectively.

Hence, the arguments a and b are required to execute function, or calling the function without the arguments would result in an error. Errors related to missing arguments could be avoided by setting default values to the arguments:

```
def add_function(a=0, b=0):
    c = a + b
    print("The sum of a and b is ", c)
```

The preceding function expects two arguments. If we pass only one argument to this function, the other defaults to zero. For example, add_function(a=3), b defaults to 0, or add_function(b=2), a defaults to 0. When an argument is not furnished while calling a function, it defaults to zero (declared in the function).

Similarly, the print function prints any variable passed as an argument. If the print function is called without any arguments, a blank line is printed.

# Returning values from a function

Functions can perform a set of defined operations and finally return a value at the end. Let's consider the following example:

```
def square(a):
    return a**2
```

In this example, the function returns a square of the argument. In Python, the return keyword is used to return a value requested upon completion of execution.

# The scope of variables in a function

There are two types of variables in a Python program: local and global variables. **Local variables** are local to a function, that is, it is a variable declared within a function is accessible within that function. The example is as follows:

```
def add_function():
    a = 3
    b = 2
    c = a + b
    print("The sum of a and b is ", c)
```

In this example, the variables a and b are local to the function `add_function`. Let's consider an example of a **global variable**:

```
a = 3
b = 2
def add_function():
    c = a + b
    print("The sum of a and b is ", c)

add_function()
```

In this case, the variables a and b are declared in the main body of the Python script. They are accessible across the entire program. Now, let's consider this example:

```
a = 3
def my_function():
    a = 5
    print("The value of a is ", a)

my_function()
print("The value of a is ", a)
```

The program output is:

```
The value of a is

5

The value of a is

3
```

In this case, when `my_function` is called, the value of a is 5 and the value of a is 3 in the `print` statement of the main body of the script. In Python, it is not possible to explicitly modify the value of global variables inside functions. In order to modify the value of a global variable, we need to make use of the `global` keyword:

```
a = 3
def my_function():
    global a
    a = 5
    print("The value of a is ", a)

my_function()
print("The value of a is ", a)
```

In general, it is not recommended to modify variables inside functions as it is not a very safe practice of modifying variables. The best practice would be passing variables as arguments and returning the modified value. Consider the following example:

```
a = 3
def my_function(a):
    a = 5
    print("The value of a is ", a)
    return a

a = my_function(a)
print("The value of a is ", a)
```

In the preceding program, the value of a is 3. It is passed as an argument to `my_function`. The function returns 5, which is saved to a. We were able to safely modify the value of a.

# GPIO callback functions

Let's review some uses of functions with the GPIO example. Functions can be used in order to handle specific events related to the GPIO pins of the Raspberry Pi. For example, the `gpiozero` library provides the capability of calling a function either when a button is pressed or released:

```
from gpiozero import Button

def button_pressed():
    print("button pressed")

def button_released():
    print("button released")
```

```
#button is interfaced to GPIO 2
button = Button(2)
button.when_pressed = button_pressed
button.when_released = button_released

while True:
  pass
```

In this example, we make use of the attributes `when_pressed` and `when_released` of the library's GPIO class. When the button is pressed, the function `button_pressed` is executed. Likewise, when the button is released, the function `button_released` is executed. We make use of the `while` loop to avoid exiting the program and keep listening for button events. The `pass` keyword is used to avoid an error and nothing happens when a `pass` keyword is executed.

This capability of being able to execute different functions for different events is useful in applications like *home automation*. For example, it could be used to turn on lights when it is dark and vice versa.

# DC motor control in Python

In this section, we will discuss motor control using the Raspberry Pi Zero. Why discuss motor control? As we progress through different topics in this book, we will culminate in building a mobile robot. Hence, we need to discuss writing code in Python to control a motor using a Raspberry Pi.

In order to control a motor, we need an **H-bridge motor driver** (Discussing H-bridge is beyond our scope. There are several resources for H-bridge motor drivers: `http://www.mcmanis.com/chuck/robotics/tutorial/h-bridge/`). There are several motor driver kits designed for the Raspberry Pi. In this section, we will make use of the following kit: `https://www.pololu.com/product/2753`.

The **Pololu** product page also provides instructions on how to connect the motor. Let's get to writing some Python code to operate the motor:

```
from gpiozero import Motor
from gpiozero import OutputDevice
import time

motor_1_direction = OutputDevice(13)
motor_2_direction = OutputDevice(12)

motor = Motor(5, 6)
```

```
motor_1_direction.on()
motor_2_direction.on()

motor.forward()

time.sleep(10)

motor.stop()

motor_1_direction.off()
motor_2_direction.off()
```

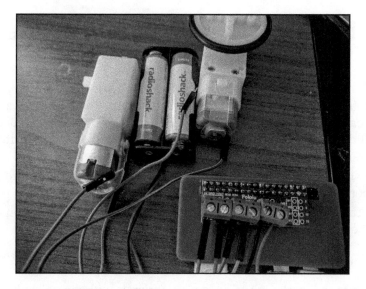

Raspberry Pi based motor control

In order to control the motor, let's declare the pins, the motor's speed pins and direction pins. As per the motor driver's documentation, the motors are controlled by GPIO pins 12, 13 and 5, 6, respectively.

```
from gpiozero import Motor
from gpiozero import OutputDevice
import time

motor_1_direction = OutputDevice(13)
motor_2_direction = OutputDevice(12)

motor = Motor(5, 6)
```

Controlling the motor is as simple as turning on the motor using the `on()` method and moving the motor in the forward direction using the `forward()` method:

```
motor.forward()
```

Similarly, reversing the motor direction could be done by calling the `reverse()` method. Stopping the motor could be done by:

```
motor.stop()
```

# Some mini-project challenges for the reader

Here are some of mini-project challenged for our readers:

- In this chapter, we discussed interfacing inputs for the Raspberry Pi and controlling motors. Think about a project where we could drive a mobile robot that reads inputs from whisker switches and operate a mobile robot. Is it possible to build a wall following robot in combination with the limit switches and motors?
- We discussed controlling a DC motor in this chapter. How do we control a stepper motor using a Raspberry Pi?
- How can we interface a motion sensor to control the lights at home using a Raspberry Pi Zero?

Read on to find out!

 Interested in playing tricks on your friends with your Raspberry Pi Zero? Check this book's website!

# Summary

In this chapter, we discussed conditional statements and the applications of conditional statements in Python. We also discussed functions in Python, passing arguments to a function, returning values from a function and scope of variables in a Python program. We discussed callback functions and motor control in Python.

# 4

# Communication Interfaces

So far, we have discussed loops, conditional statements, and functions in Python. We also discussed interfacing output devices and simple digital input devices.

In this chapter, we will discuss the following communication interfaces:

- UART – serial port
- Serial Peripheral Interface
- I²C interface

 We will be making use of different sensors/electronic components to demonstrate writing code in Python for these interfaces. We leave it up to you to pick a component of your choice to explore these communication interfaces.

## UART – serial port

**Universal Asynchronous Receiver/Transmitter (UART)**, a serial port, is a communication interface where the data is transmitted serially in bits from a sensor to the host computer. Using a serial port is one of the oldest forms of communication protocol. It is used in data logging where microcontrollers collect data from sensors and transmit the data via a serial port. There are also sensors that transmit data via serial communication as responses to incoming commands.

We will not go into the theory behind serial port communications (there's plenty of theory available on the Web at
`https://en.wikipedia.org/wiki/Universal_asynchronous_receiver/transmitter`). We will be discussing the use of the serial port to interface different sensors with the Raspberry Pi.

# Raspberry Pi Zero's UART port

Typically, UART ports consist of a receiver (*Rx*) and a transmitter (*Tx*) pin that receive and transmit data. The Raspberry Pi's GPIO header comes with an UART port. The GPIO pins 14 (the *Tx* pin) and 15 (is the *Rx* pin) serve as the UART port for the Raspberry Pi:

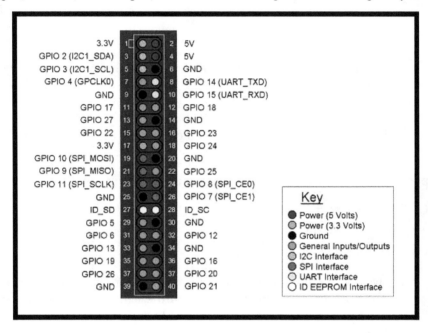

GPIO pins 14 and 15 are the UART pins (image source: https://www.rs-online.com/designspark/introducing-the-raspberry-pi-b-plus)

# Setting up the Raspberry Pi Zero serial port

In order to use the serial port to talk to sensors, the serial port login/console needs to be disabled. In the **Raspbian** OS image, this is enabled by default as it enables easy debugging.

The serial port login can be disabled via `raspi-config`:

1. Launch the terminal and run this command:

```
sudo raspi-config
```

2. Select **Advanced Options** from the main menu of `raspi-config`:

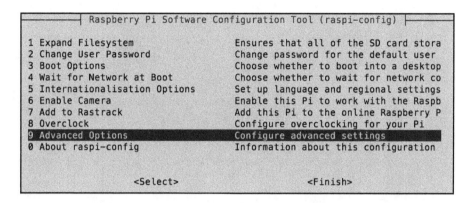

Select Advanced Options from the raspi-config menu

3. Select the **A8 Serial** option from the drop-down menu:

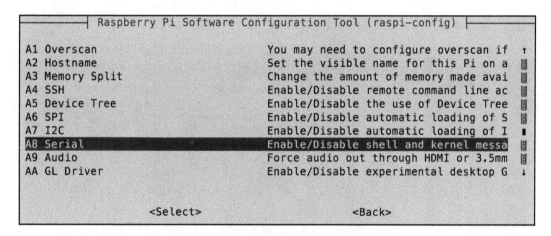

Select A8 Serial from the dropdown

4. Disable serial login:

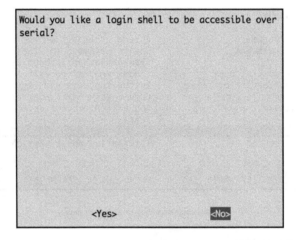

Disable serial login

5. Finish the configuration and reboot at the end:

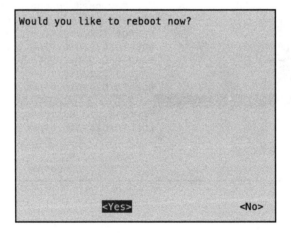

Save config and reboot

# Example 1 – interfacing a carbon dioxide sensor to the Raspberry Pi

We will be making use of the K30 carbon dioxide sensor (its documentation is available here, `http://co2meters.com/Documentation/Datasheets/DS30-01%20-%20K30.pdf`). It has a range of 0-10,000 ppm, and the sensor provides it carbon dioxide concentration readings via serial port as a response to certain commands from the Raspberry Pi.

The following diagram shows the connections between the Raspberry Pi and the K30 carbon dioxide sensor:

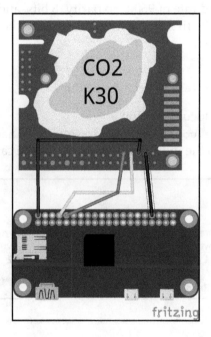

K30 carbon dioxide sensor interfaced with the Raspberry Pi

The receiver (*Rx*) pin of the sensor is connected to the transmitter (*Tx*-**GPIO 14 (UART_TXD)**) pin of the Raspberry Pi Zero (the yellow wire in the preceding figure). The transmitter (*Tx*) pin of the sensor is connected to the receiver (*Rx*-**GPIO 15 (UART_RXD)**) pin of the Raspberry Pi Zero (the green wire in the preceding figure).

In order to power the sensor, the G+ pin of the sensor (the red wire in the preceding figure) is connected to the **5V** pin of the Raspberry Pi Zero. The G0 pin of the sensor is connected to the **GND** pin of the Raspberry Pi Zero (black wire in the earlier figure).

Typically, serial port communication is initiated by specifying the baud rate, the number of bits in a frame, stop bit, and flow control.

# Python code for serial port communication

We will make use of the **pySerial** library (https://pyserial.readthedocs.io/en/latest/shortintro.html#opening-serial-ports) for interfacing the carbon dioxide sensor:

1. As per the sensor's documentation, the sensor output can be read by initiating the serial port at a baud rate of 9600, no parity, 8 bits, and 1 stop bit. The GPIO serial port is ttyAMA0. The first step in interfacing with the sensor is initiating serial port communication:

```
import serial
ser = serial.Serial("/dev/ttyAMA0")
```

2. As per the sensor documentation (http://co2meters.com/Documentation/Other/SenseAirCommGuide.zip), the sensor responds to the following command for the carbon dioxide concentration:

**Reading CO2**

**Request:**

| Description | Address 1byte | Command 1-byte | Address (see I2C guide) 2-bytes | | N- Bytes to Read 1-byte | Checksum 2-bytes | |
|---|---|---|---|---|---|---|---|
| Example (reads CO2) | 0xFE | 0x44 | 0x00 | 0x08 | 0x02 | 0x9F | 0x25 |
| Command Bytes: 0x46- EEPROM Read, 0x44 – RAM Read | | | | | | | |

Command to read carbon dioxide concentration from the sensor-borrowed from the sensor datasheet

3. The command can be transmitted to the sensor as follows:

```
ser.write(bytearray([0xFE, 0x44, 0x00, 0x08, 0x02, 0x9F, 0x25]))
```

4. The sensor responds with a 7-byte response, which can be read as follows:

```
resp = ser.read(7)
```

5. The sensor's response is in the following format:

**Response**

| Description | Address 1byte | Command 1-byte | Count 1-byte | N- Bytes Read n-bytes | | Checksum 2-bytes | |
|---|---|---|---|---|---|---|---|
| **Example (cont.)** | 0xFE | 0x44 | 0x02 | 0x01 | 0x90 | | |

Carbon dioxide sensor response

6. According to the datasheet, the sensor data size is 2 bytes. Each byte can be used to store a value of 0 and 255. Two bytes can be used to store values up to 65,535 (255 * 255). The carbon dioxide concentration could be calculated from the message as follows:

```
high = resp[3]
low = resp[4]
co2 = (high*256) + low
```

7. Put it all together:

```
import serial
import time
import array
ser = serial.Serial("/dev/ttyAMA0")
print("Serial Connected!")
ser.flushInput()
time.sleep(1)

while True:
    ser.write(bytearray([0xFE, 0x44, 0x00, 0x08,
    0x02, 0x9F, 0x25]))
    # wait for sensor to respond
    time.sleep(.01)
    resp = ser.read(7)
    high = resp[3]
    low = resp[4]
    co2 = (high*256) + low
    print()
    print()
    print("Co2 = " + str(co2))
    time.sleep(1)
```

8. Save the code to a file and try executing it.

# I2C communication

**Inter-Integrated Circuit** ($I^2C$) communication is a type of serial communication that allows interfacing multiple sensors to the computer. $I^2C$ communication consists of two wires of a clock and a data line. The Raspberry Pi Zero's clock and data pins for $I^2C$ communication are **GPIO 3 (SCL)** and **GPIO 2 (SDA)**, respectively. In order to communicate with multiple sensors over the same bus, sensors/actuators that communicate via $I^2C$ protocol are usually addressed by their 7-bit address. It is possible to have two or more Raspberry Pi boards talking to the same sensor on the same $I^2C$ bus. This enables building a sensor network around the Raspberry Pi.

The $I^2C$ communication lines are open drain lines; hence, they are pulled up using resistors, as shown in the following figure:

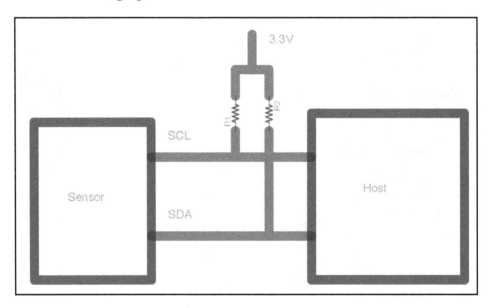

$I^2C$ setup

Let's review an example of $I^2C$ communication using an example.

# Example 2 – PiGlow

The **PiGlow** is a piece of add-on hardware for the Raspberry Pi that consists of 18 LEDs interfaced with the **SN3218** chip. This chip permits controlling the LEDs via the $I^2C$ interface. The chip's 7-bit address is 0x54.

To interface the add-on hardware, the **SCL** pin is connected to **GPIO 3** and **SDA** pin to **GPIO 2**; the ground pins and the power supply pins are connected to the counterparts of the add-on hardware, respectively.

The PiGlow comes with a library that comes which abstracts the I²C communication: `https://github.com/pimoroni/piglow`.

Although the library is a wrapper around the I²C interface for the library, we recommend reading through the code to understand the internal mechanism to operate the LEDs:

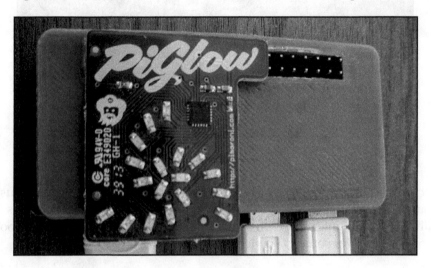

PiGlow stacked on top of the Raspberry Pi

# Installing libraries

The PiGlow library may be installed by running the following from the command-line terminal:

```
curl get.pimoroni.com/piglow | bash
```

# Example

On the completion of installation, switch to the example folder (`/home/pi/Pimoroni/piglow`) and run one of the examples:

```
python3 bar.py
```

It should run *blinky* light effects as shown in the following figure:

Blinky lights on the PiGlow

Similarly, there are libraries to talk to real-time clocks, LCD displays, and so on using I²C communication. If you are interested in writing your own interface that provides the nitty-gritty detail of I²C communication with sensors/output devices, check out this book's accompanying website for some examples.

# Example 3 – Sensorian add-on hardware for the Raspberry Pi

The **Sensorian** is an add-on hardware designed for the Raspberry Pi. This add-on hardware comes with different types of sensors, including a light sensor, barometer, accelerometer, LCD display interface, flash memory, capacitive touch sensors, and a real-time clock.

The sensors on this add-on hardware is sufficient to learn using all the communication interfaces discussed in this chapter:

Sensorian hardware stacked on top of the Raspberry Pi Zero

In this section, we will discuss an example where we will measure the ambient light levels using a Raspberry Pi Zero via the I²C interface. The sensor on the add-on hardware board is the **APDS-9300** sensor (www.avagotech.com/docs/AV02-1077EN).

## I2C drivers for the lux sensor

The drivers are available from the GitHub repository for the Sensorian hardware (https://github.com/sensorian/sensorian-firmware.git). Let's clone the repository from the command-line terminal:

```
git clone https://github.com/sensorian/sensorian-firmware.git
```

Let's make use of the drivers (which is available in the `~/sensorian-firmware/Drivers_Python/APDS-9300` folder) to read the values from the two ADC channels of the sensor:

```
import time
import APDS9300 as LuxSens
import sys

AmbientLight = LuxSens.APDS9300()
while True:
    time.sleep(1)
    channel1 = AmbientLight.readChannel(1)
    channel2 = AmbientLight.readChannel(0)
    Lux = AmbientLight.getLuxLevel(channel1,channel2)
    print("Lux output: %d." % Lux)
```

With the ADC values available from both the channel, the ambient light value can be calculated by the driver using the following formula (retrieved from the sensor datasheet):

| CH1/CH0 | Sensor Lux Formula |
|---|---|
| 0 ≤ CH1/CH0 ≤ 0.52 | Sensor Lux = (0.0315 x CH0) – (0.0593 x CH0 x ((CH1/CH0)$^{1.4}$)) |
| 0.52 ≤ CH1/CH0 ≤ 0.65 | Sensor Lux = (0.0229 x CH0) – (0.0291 x CH1) |
| 0.65 ≤ CH1/CH0 ≤ 0.80 | Sensor Lux = (0.0157 x CH0) – (0.0180 x CH1) |
| 0.80 ≤ CH1/CH0 ≤ 1.30 | Sensor Lux = (0.00338 x CH0) – (0.00260 x CH1) |
| CH1/CH0 ≥ 1.30 | Sensor Lux = 0 |

Ambient light levels calculated using the ADC values

This calculation is performed by the attribute `getLuxLevel`. Under normal lighting conditions, the ambient light level (measured in lux) was around 2. The measured output was 0 when we covered the lux sensor with the palm. This sensor could be used to measure ambient light and adjust the room lighting accordingly.

## Challenge

We discussed measuring ambient light levels using the lux sensor. How do we make use of the lux output (ambient light levels) to control the room lighting?

# The SPI interface

There is another type of serial communication interface named the **Serial Peripheral Interface** (**SPI**). This interface has to be enabled via `raspi-config` (this is similar to enabling serial port interface earlier in this chapter). Using the SPI interface is similar to that of I²C interface and the serial port.

Typically, an SPI interface consists of a clock line, data-in, data-out, and a **Slave Select** (**SS**) line. Unlike I²C communication (where we could connect multiple masters), there can be only one master (the Raspberry Pi Zero), but multiple slaves on the same bus. The **SS** pin enables selecting a specific sensor that the Raspberry Pi Zero is reading/writing data when there are multiple sensors connected to the same bus.

# Example 4 – writing to external memory chip

Let's review an example where we write to a flash memory chip on the Sensorian add-on hardware via the SPI interface. The drivers for the SPI interface and the memory chip are available from the same GitHub repository.

Since we already have the drivers downloaded, let's review an example available with drivers:

```
import sys
import time
import S25FL204K as Memory
```

Let's initialize and write the message `hello` to the memory:

```
Flash_memory = Memory.S25FL204K()
Flash_memory.writeStatusRegister(0x00)
message = "hello"
flash_memory.writeArray(0x000000,list(message), message.len())
```

Now, let's try to read the data we just wrote to the external memory:

```
data = flash_memory.readArray(0x000000, message.len())
print("Data Read from memory: ")
print(''.join(data))
```

The code sample is available for download with this chapter (`memory_test.py`).

We were able to demonstrate using the SPI to read/write to an external memory chip.

## Challenge to the reader

In the figure here, there is an LED strip (`https://www.adafruit.com/product/306`) interfaced to the SPI interface of the Raspberry Pi add on hardware using the Adafruit Cobbler (`https://www.adafruit.com/product/914`). We are providing a clue on how to interface the LED strip to the Raspberry Pi Zero. We would like to see if you are able to find a solution to interface the LED strip by yourself. Refer to this book's website for the answer.

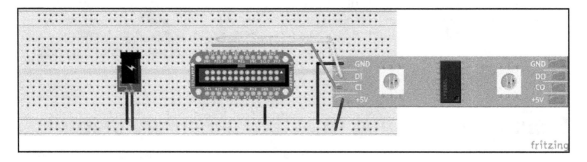

LED strip interfaced with the Adafruit Cobbler for the Raspberry Pi Zero

# Summary

In this chapter, we have discussed different communication interfaces that are available on the Raspberry Pi Zero. These interfaces include I²C, SPI, and UART. We will be making use of these interfaces in our final projects. We discussed these interfaces using a carbon dioxide sensor, LED driver, and a sensor platform. In the next chapter, we will discuss object-oriented programming and its distinct advantages. We will discuss the need for object-oriented programming using an example. Object-oriented programming can be especially helpful in scenarios where you have to write your own drivers to control a component of your robot or write an interface library for a sensor.

# 5

# Data Types and Object-Oriented Programming in Python

In this chapter, we will discuss data types and **object-oriented programming** (OOP) in Python. We will discuss data types including lists, dictionaries, tuples and sets in Python. We will also discuss OOP, it's necessity and how to write object-oriented code in Python for Raspberry Pi based projects (such as, using OOP to control appliances at home). We will discuss making use of OOP in a Raspberry Pi Zero project.

## Lists

In Python, a list is a data type (its documentation is available here, `https://docs.python.o rg/3.4/tutorial/datastructures.html#`) that could be used to store elements in a sequence.

 The topics discussed in this chapter can be difficult to grasp unless used in practice. Any example that is represented using this notation: >>> indicates that it could be tested using the Python interpreter.

A list may consist of strings, objects (discussed in detail in this chapter) or numbers, and so on. For instance, the following are examples of lists:

```
>>> sequence = [1, 2, 3, 4, 5, 6]
>>> example_list = ['apple', 'orange', 1.0, 2.0, 3]
```

In the preceding set of examples, the `sequence` list consists of numbers between 1 and 6 while the `example_list` list consists of a combination of strings, integer, and floating-point numbers. A list is represented by square brackets (`[]`). Items can be added to a list separated by commas:

```
>>> type(sequence)
<class 'list'>
```

Since a list is an ordered sequence of elements, the elements of a list could be fetched by iterating through the list elements using a `for` loop as follows:

```
for item in sequence:
    print("The number is ", item)
```

The output is something as follows:

```
The number is  1
The number is  2
The number is  3
The number is  4
The number is  5
The number is  6
```

Since Python's loop can iterate through a sequence of elements, it fetches each element and assigns it to `item`. This item is printed on the console.

# Operations that could be performed on a list

In Python, the attributes of a data type can be retrieved using the `dir()` method. For example, the attributes available for the `sequence` list can be retrieved as follows:

```
>>> dir(sequence)
['__add__', '__class__', '__contains__', '__delattr__',
'__delitem__', '__dir__', '__doc__', '__eq__',
'__format__', '__ge__', '__getattribute__', '__getitem__',
'__gt__', '__hash__', '__iadd__', '__imul__', '__init__',
'__iter__', '__le__', '__len__', '__lt__', '__mul__',
'__ne__', '__new__', '__reduce__', '__reduce_ex__',
'__repr__', '__reversed__', '__rmul__', '__setattr__',
'__setitem__', '__sizeof__', '__str__', '__subclasshook__',
'append', 'clear', 'copy', 'count', 'extend', 'index',
'insert', 'pop', 'remove', 'reverse', 'sort']
```

These attributes enable performing different operations on a list. Let's discuss each attribute in detail.

# Append element to list:

It is possible to add an element using the append() method:

```
>>> sequence.append(7)
>>> sequence
[1, 2, 3, 4, 5, 6, 7]
```

# Remove element from list:

The remove() method finds the first instance of the element (passed an argument) and removes it from the list. Let's consider the following examples:

- Example 1:

```
>>> sequence = [1, 1, 2, 3, 4, 7, 5, 6, 7]
>>> sequence.remove(7)
>>> sequence
[1, 1, 2, 3, 4, 5, 6, 7]
```

- Example 2:

```
>>> sequence.remove(1)
>>> sequence
[1, 2, 3, 4, 5, 6, 7]
```

- Example 3:

```
>>> sequence.remove(1)
>>> sequence
[2, 3, 4, 5, 6, 7]
```

# Retrieving the index of an element

The index() method returns the position of an element in a list:

```
>>> index_list = [1, 2, 3, 4, 5, 6, 7]
>>> index_list.index(5)
4
```

In this example, the method returns the index of the element 5. Since Python uses zero-based indexing that is the index is counted from 0 and hence the index of the element 5 is 4:

```
random_list = [2, 2, 4, 5, 5, 5, 6, 7, 7, 8]
>>> random_list.index(5)
3
```

In this example, the method returns the position of the first instance of the element. The element 5 is located at the third position.

# Popping an element from the list

The pop() method enables removing an element from a specified position and return it:

```
>>> index_list = [1, 2, 3, 4, 5, 6, 7]
>>> index_list.pop(3)
4
>>> index_list
[1, 2, 3, 5, 6, 7]
```

In this example, the index_list list consists of numbers between 1 and 7. When the third element is popped by passing the index position (3) as an argument, the number 4 is removed from the list and returned.

If no arguments are provided for the index position, the last element is popped and returned:

```
>>> index_list.pop()
7
>>> index_list
[1, 2, 3, 5, 6]
```

In this example, the last element (7) was popped and returned.

# Counting the instances of an element:

The count() method returns the number of times an element appears in a list. For example, the element appears twice in the list: random_list.

```
>>> random_list = [2, 9, 8, 4, 3, 2, 1, 7]
>>> random_list.count(2)
2
```

# Inserting element at a specific position:

The `insert()` method enables adding an element at a specific position in the list. For example, let's consider the following example:

```
>>> day_of_week = ['Monday', 'Tuesday', 'Thursday',
'Friday', 'Saturday']
```

In the list, `Wednesday` is missing. It needs to be positioned between `Tuesday` and `Thursday` at position 2 (Python uses **zero based indexing** that is the positions/indexes of elements are counted as 0, 1, 2, and so on.). It could be added using insert as follows:

```
>>> day_of_week.insert(2, 'Wednesday')
>>> day_of_week
['Monday', 'Tuesday', 'Wednesday', 'Thursday',
'Friday', 'Saturday']
```

## Challenge to the reader

In the preceding list, `Sunday` is missing. Use the `insert` attribute of lists to insert it at the correct position.

# Extending a list

Two lists can be combined together using the `extend()` method. The `day_of_week` and `sequence` lists can be combined as follows:

```
>>> day_of_week.extend(sequence)
>>> day_of_week
['Monday', 'Tuesday', 'Wednesday', 'Thursday', 'Friday',
'Saturday', 1, 2, 3, 4, 5, 6]
```

Lists can also be combined as follows:

```
>>> [1, 2, 3] + [4, 5, 6]
[1, 2, 3, 4, 5, 6]
```

It is also possible to add a list as an element to another list:

```
sequence.insert(6, [1, 2, 3])
>>> sequence
[1, 2, 3, 4, 5, 6, [1, 2, 3]]
```

# Clearing the elements of a list

All the elements of a list could be deleted using the `clear()` method:

```
>>> sequence.clear()
>>> sequence
[]
```

# Sorting the elements of a list

The elements of a list could be sorted using the `sort()` method:

```
random_list = [8, 7, 5, 2, 2, 5, 7, 5, 6, 4]
>>> random_list.sort()
>>> random_list
[2, 2, 4, 5, 5, 5, 6, 7, 7, 8]
```

When a list consists of a collection of strings, they are sorted in the alphabetical order:

```
>>> day_of_week = ['Monday', 'Tuesday', 'Thursday',
'Friday', 'Saturday']
>>> day_of_week.sort()
>>> day_of_week
['Friday', 'Monday', 'Saturday', 'Thursday', 'Tuesday']
```

# Reverse the order of elements in list

The `reverse()` method enables the reversing the order of the list elements:

```
>>> random_list = [8, 7, 5, 2, 2, 5, 7, 5, 6, 4]
>>> random_list.reverse()
>>> random_list
[4, 6, 5, 7, 5, 2, 2, 5, 7, 8]
```

# Create copies of a list

The `copy()` method enables creating copies of a list:

```
>>> copy_list = random_list.copy()
>>> copy_list
[4, 6, 5, 7, 5, 2, 2, 5, 7, 8]
```

# Accessing list elements

The list elements could be accessed by specifying the index position of the `list_name[i]` element. For example, the zeroth list element of the `random_list` list could be accessed as follows:

```
>>> random_list = [4, 6, 5, 7, 5, 2, 2, 5, 7, 8]
>>> random_list[0]4>>> random_list[3]7
```

## Accessing a set of elements within a list

It is possible to access elements between specified indices. For example, it is possible to retrieve all elements between indices 2 and 4:

```
>>> random_list[2:5]
[5, 7, 5]
```

The first six elements of a list could be accessed as follows:

```
>>> random_list[:6]
[4, 6, 5, 7, 5, 2]
```

The elements of a list could be printed in the reverse order as follows:

```
>>> random_list[::-1]
[8, 7, 5, 2, 2, 5, 7, 5, 6, 4]
```

Every second element in the list could be fetched as follows:

```
>>> random_list[::2]
[4, 5, 5, 2, 7]
```

It is also possible to fetch every second element after the second element after skipping the first two elements:

```
>>> random_list[2::2]
[5, 5, 2, 7]
```

# List membership

It is possible to check if a value is a member of a list using the `in` keyword. For example:

```
>>> random_list = [2, 1, 0, 8, 3, 1, 10, 9, 5, 4]
```

In this list, we could check if the number 6 is a member:

```
>>> 6 in random_list
False
>>> 4 in random_list
True
```

# Let's build a simple game!

This exercise consists of two parts. In the first part, we will review building a list containing ten random numbers between 0 and 10. The second part is a challenge to the reader. Perform the following steps:

1. The first step is creating an empty list. Let's create an empty list called random_list. An empty list can be created as follows:

   ```
   random_list = []
   ```

2. We will be making use of Python's random module (https://docs.python.org/3/library/random.html) to generate random numbers. In order to generate random numbers between 0 and 10, we will make use of the randint() method from the random module:

   ```
   random_number = random.randint(0,10)
   ```

3. Let's append the generated number to the list. This operation is repeated 10 times using a for loop:

   ```
   for index in range(0,10):
           random_number = random.randint(0, 10)
           random_list.append(random_number)
   print("The items in random_list are ")
   print(random_list)
   ```

4. The generated list looks something like this:

   ```
   The items in random_list are
   [2, 1, 0, 8, 3, 1, 10, 9, 5, 4]
   ```

We discussed generating a list of random numbers. The next step is taking user input where we ask the user to make a guess for a number between 0 and 10. If the number is a member of the list, the message Your guess is correct is printed to the screen, else, the message Sorry! Your guess is incorrect is printed. We leave the second part as a challenge to the reader. Get started with the list_generator.py code sample available for download with this chapter.

# Dictionaries

A dictionary (https://docs.python.org/3.4/tutorial/datastructures.html#dictionaries) is a data type that is an unordered collection of key and value pairs. Each key in a dictionary has an associated value. An example of a dictionary is:

```
>>> my_dict = {1: "Hello", 2: "World"}
>>> my_dict
{1: 'Hello', 2: 'World'}
```

A dictionary is created by using the braces { }. At the time of creation, new members are added to the dictionary in the following format: key: value (shown in the preceding example). In the previous example 1 and 2 are keys while 'Hello' and 'World' are the associated values. Each value added to a dictionary needs to have an associated key.

The elements of a dictionary do not have an order i.e. the elements cannot be retrieved in the order they were added. It is possible to retrieving the values of a dictionary by iterating through the keys. Let's consider the following example:

```
>>> my_dict = {1: "Hello", 2: "World", 3: "I", 4: "am",
5: "excited", 6: "to", 7: "learn", 8: "Python" }
```

There are several ways to print the keys or values of a dictionary:

```
>>> for key in my_dict:

...

print(my_dict[value])

...

Hello

World
```

```
I

am

excited

to

learn

Python
```

In the preceding example, we iterate through the keys of the dictionary and retrieve the value using the key, `my_dict [key]`. It is also possible to retrieve the values using the `values ()` method available with dictionaries:

```
>>> for value in my_dict.values():

...

print(value)

...

Hello

World

I

am

excited

to

learn

Python
```

The keys of a dictionary can be an integer, string, or a tuple. The keys of a dictionary need to be unique and it is immutable, that is a key cannot be modified after creation. Duplicates of a key cannot be created. If a new value is added to an existing key, the latest value is stored in the dictionary. Let's consider the following example:

- A new key/value pair could be added to a dictionary as follows:

```
>>> my_dict[9] = 'test'

>>> my_dict

{1: 'Hello', 2: 'World', 3: 'I', 4: 'am', 5: 'excited',
6: 'to', 7: 'learn', 8: 'Python', 9: 'test'}
```

- Let's try creating a duplicate of the key 9:

```
>>> my_dict[9] = 'programming'

>>> my_dict

{1: 'Hello', 2: 'World', 3: 'I', 4: 'am', 5: 'excited',
6: 'to', 7: 'learn', 8: 'Python', 9: 'programming'}
```

- As shown in the preceding example, when we try to create a duplicate, the value of the existing key is modified.
- It is possible to have multiple values associated with a key. For example, as a list or a dictionary:

```
>>> my_dict = {1: "Hello", 2: "World", 3: "I", 4: "am",
"values": [1, 2, 3,4, 5], "test": {"1": 1, "2": 2} }
```

Dictionaries are useful in scenarios like parsing CSV files and associating each row with a unique key. Dictionaries are also used to encode and decode JSON data

# Tuples

A tuple (pronounced either like *two-ple* or *tuh-ple*) is an immutable data type that are ordered and separated by a comma. A tuple can be created as follows:

```
>>> my_tuple = 1, 2, 3, 4, 5

>>> my_tuple

(1, 2, 3, 4, 5)
```

Since tuples are immutable, the value at a given index cannot be modified:

```
>>> my_tuple[1] = 3
Traceback (most recent call last):
  File "<stdin>", line 1, in <module>
TypeError: 'tuple' object does not support item assignment
```

A tuple can consist of a number, string, or a list. Since lists are mutable, if a list is a member of a tuple, it can be modified. For example:

```
>>> my_tuple = 1, 2, 3, 4, [1, 2, 4, 5]
>>> my_tuple[4][2] = 3
>>> my_tuple
(1, 2, 3, 4, [1, 2, 3, 5])
```

Tuples are especially useful in scenarios where the value cannot be modified. Tuples are also used to return values from a function. Let's consider the following example:

```
>>> for value in my_dict.items():

...

print(value)

...

(1, 'Hello')

(2, 'World')

(3, 'I')

(4, 'am')

('test', {'1': 1, '2': 2})

('values', [1, 2, 3, 4, 5])
```

In the preceding example, the items() method returns a list of tuples.

# Sets

A set (https://docs.python.org/3/tutorial/datastructures.html#sets) is an unordered collection of immutable elements without duplicate entries. A set could be created as follows:

```
>>> my_set = set([1, 2, 3, 4, 5])

>>> my_set

{1, 2, 3, 4, 5}
```

Now, let's add a duplicate list to this set:

```
>>> my_set.update([1, 2, 3, 4, 5])

>>> my_set

{1, 2, 3, 4, 5}
```

Sets enable avoid duplication of entries and saving the unique entries. A single element can be added to a set as follows:

```
>>> my_set = set([1, 2, 3, 4, 5])

>>> my_set.add(6)

>>> my_set

{1, 2, 3, 4, 5, 6}
```

Sets are used to test memberships of an element among different sets. There are different methods that are related to membership tests. We recommend learning about each method using the documentation on sets (run `help(my_set)` to find the different methods available for membership tests).

# OOP in Python

OOP is a concept that helps simplifying your code and eases application development. It is especially useful in reusing your code. Object-oriented code enables reusing your code for sensors that use the communications interface. For example, all sensors that are equipped with a UART port could be grouped together using object-oriented code.

One example of OOP is the **GPIO Zero library**
(https://www.raspberrypi.org/blog/gpio-zero-a-friendly-python-api-for-physical-computing/) used in previous chapters. In fact, everything is an object in Python.

Object-oriented code is especially helpful in collaboration with other people on a project. For example, you could implement a sensor driver using object-oriented code in Python and document its usage. This enables other developers to develop an application without paying attention to the nitty-gritty detail behind the sensor's interface. OOP provides modularity to an application that simplifies application development. We are going to review an example in this chapter that demonstrates the advantage of OOP. In this chapter, we will be making use of OOP to bring modularity to our project.

Let's get started!

# Revisiting the student ID card example

Let's revisit the ID card example from Chapter 2, *Arithmetic Operations, Loops, and Blinky Lights* (input_test.py). We discussed writing a simple program that captures and prints the information belonging to a student. A student's contact information could be retrieved and stored as follows:

```
name = input("What is your name? ")
address = input("What is your address? ")
age = input("How old are you? ")
```

Now, consider a scenario where the information of 10 students has to be saved and retrieved at any point during program execution. We would need to come up with a nomenclature for the variables used to save the student information. It would be a clutter if we use 30 different variables to store information belonging to each student. This is where object oriented programming can be really helpful.

Let's rewrite this example using OOP to simplify the problem. The first step in OOP is declaring a structure for the object. This is done by defining a class. The class determines the functions of an object. Let's write a Python class that defines the structure for a student object.

# Class

Since we are going to save student information, the class is going to be called Student. A class is defined using the class keyword as follows:

```
class Student(object):
```

Thus, a class called Student has been defined. Whenever a new object is created, the method __init__() (the underscore indicate that the init method is a magic method, that is it is a function that is called by Python when an object is created) is called internally by Python.

This method is defined within the class:

```python
class Student(object):
    """A Python class to store student information"""

    def __init__(self, name, address, age):
        self.name = name
        self.address = address
        self.age = age
```

In this example, the arguments to the __init__ method include name, age and address. These arguments are called **attributes**. These attributes enable creating a unique object that belongs to the Student class. Hence, in this example, while creating an instance of the Student class, the attributes name, age, and address are required arguments.

Let's create an object (also called an instance) belonging to the Student class:

```python
student1 = Student("John Doe", "123 Main Street, Newark, CA", "29")
```

In this example, we created an object belonging to the Student class called student1 where John Doe (name), 29 (age) and 123 Main Street, Newark, CA(address) are attributes required to create an object. When we create an object that belongs to the Student class by passing the requisite arguments (declared earlier in the __init__() method of the Student class), the __init__() method is automatically called to initialize the object. Upon initialization, the information related to student1 is stored under the object student1.

Now, the information belonging to student1 could be retrieved as follows:

```python
print(student1.name)
print(student1.age)
print(student1.address)
```

Now, let's create another object called student2:

```python
student2 = Student("Jane Doe", "123 Main Street, San Jose, CA", "27")
```

We created two objects called `student1` and `student2`. Each object's attributes are accessible as `student1.name`, `student2.name` and so on. In the absence of object oriented programming, we will have to create variables like `student1_name`, `student1_age`, `student1_address`, `student2_name`, `student2_age` and `student2_address` and so on. Thus, OOP enables modularizing the code.

## Adding methods to a class

Let's add some methods to our `Student` class that would help retrieve a student's information:

```python
class Student(object):
    """A Python class to store student information"""

    def __init__(self, name, age, address):
        self.name = name
        self.address = address
        self.age = age

    def return_name(self):
        """return student name"""
        return self.name

    def return_age(self):
        """return student age"""
        return self.age

    def return_address(self):
        """return student address"""
        return self.address
```

In this example, we have added three methods namely `return_name()`, `return_age()` and `return_address()` that returns the attributes `name`, `age` and `address` respectively. These methods of a class are called **callable attributes**. Let's review a quick example where we make use of these callable attributes to print an object's information.

```python
student1 = Student("John Doe", "29", "123 Main Street, Newark, CA")
print(student1.return_name())
print(student1.return_age())
print(student1.return_address())
```

So far, we discussed methods that retrieves information about a student. Let's include a method in our class that enables updating information belonging to a student. Now, let's add another method to the class that enables updating address by a student:

```
def update_address(self, address):
    """update student address"""
    self.address = address
    return self.address
```

Let's compare the `student1` object's address before and after updating the address:

```
print(student1.address())
print(student1.update_address("234 Main Street, Newark, CA"))
```

This would print the following output to your screen:

```
123 Main Street, Newark, CA
234 Main Street, Newark, CA
```

Thus, we have written our first object-oriented code that demonstrates the ability to modularize the code. The preceding code sample is available for download along with this chapter as `student_info.py`.

# Doc strings in Python

In the object oriented example, you might have noticed a sentence enclosed in triple double quotes:

```
"""A Python class to store student information"""
```

This is called a **doc string**. The doc string is used to document information about a class or a method. Doc strings are especially helpful while trying to store information related to the usage of a method or a class (this will be demonstrated later in this chapter). Doc strings are also used at the beginning of a file to store multi-line comments related to an application or a code sample. Doc strings are ignored by the Python interpreter and they are meant to provide documentation about a class to fellow programmers.

Similarly, the Python interpreter ignores any single line comment that starts with a # sign. Single line comments are generally used to make a specific note on a block of code. The practice of including well-structured comments makes your code readable.

For example, the following code snippet informs the reader that a random number between 0 and 9 is generated and stored in the variable `rand_num`:

```
# generate a random number between 0 and 9
rand_num = random.randrange(0,10)
```

On the contrary, a comment that provides no context is going to confuse someone who is reviewing your code:

```
# Todo: Fix this later
```

It is quite possible that you may not be able to recall what needs fixing when you revisit the code later.

## self

In our object-oriented example, the first argument to every method had an argument called `self`. `self` refers to the instance of the class in use and the `self` keyword is used as the first argument in methods that interact with the instances of the class. In the preceding example, `self` refers to the object `student1`. It is equivalent to initializing an object and accessing it as follows:

```
Student(student1, "John Doe", "29", "123 Main Street, Newark, CA")
Student.return_address(student1)
```

The `self` keyword simplifies how we access an object's attributes in this case. Now, let's review some examples where we make use of OOP involving the Raspberry Pi.

# Speaker controller

Let's write a Python class (`tone_player.py` in **downloads**) that plays a musical tone indicating that the boot-up of your Raspberry Pi is complete. For this section, you will need a USB sound card and a speaker interfaced to the USB hub of the Raspberry Pi.

Let's call our class `TonePlayer`. This class should be capable of controlling the speaker volume and playing any file passed as an argument while creating an object:

```
class TonePlayer(object):
    """A Python class to play boot-up complete tone"""

    def __init__(self, file_name):
        self.file_name = file_name
```

In this case, the file that has to be played by the `TonePlayer` class has to be passed an argument. For example:

```
tone_player = TonePlayer("/home/pi/tone.wav")
```

We also need to be able to set the volume level at which the tone has to be played. Let's add a method to do the same:

```
def set_volume(self, value):
    """set tone sound volume"""
    subprocess.Popen(["amixer", "set", "'PCM'", str(value)],
    shell=False)
```

In the `set_volume` method, we make use of Python's `subprocess` module to run the Linux system command that adjusts the sound drive volume.

The most essential method for this class is the `play` command. When the `play` method is called, we need to play the tone sound using Linux's a `play` command:

```
def play(self):
    """play the wav file"""
    subprocess.Popen(["aplay", self.file_name], shell=False)
```

Put it all together:

```
import subprocess

class TonePlayer(object):
    """A Python class to play boot-up complete tone"""

    def __init__(self, file_name):
        self.file_name = file_name

    def set_volume(self, value):
        """set tone sound volume"""
        subprocess.Popen(["amixer", "set", "'PCM'", str(value)],
        shell=False)

    def play(self):
        """play the wav file"""
        subprocess.Popen(["aplay", self.file_name], shell=False)


if __name__ == "__main__":
    tone_player = TonePlayer("/home/pi/tone.wav")
    tone_player.set_volume(75)
    tone_player.play()
```

Save the `TonePlayer` class to your Raspberry Pi (save it to a file called `tone_player.py`) and use a tone sound file from sources like *freesound* (`https://www.freesound.org/people/zippi1/sounds/18872/`). Save it to a location of your choice and try running the code. It should play the tone sound at the desired volume!

Now, edit `/etc/rc.local` and add the following line to the end of the file (right before the `exit 0` line):

```
python3 /home/pi/toneplayer.py
```

This should play a tone whenever the Pi boots up!

# Light control daemon

Let's review another example where we implement a simple daemon using OOP that turns on/off lights at specified times of the day. In order to be able to perform tasks at scheduled times, we will make use of the `schedule` library (`https://github.com/dbader/schedule`). It could be installed as follows:

```
sudo pip3 install schedule
```

Let's call our class, `LightScheduler`. It should be capable of accepting start and top times to turn on/off lights at given times. It should also provide override capabilities to let the user turn on/off lights as necessary. Let's assume that the light is controlled using **PowerSwitch Tail II** (`http://www.powerswitchtail.com/Pages/default.aspx`). It is interfaced as follows:

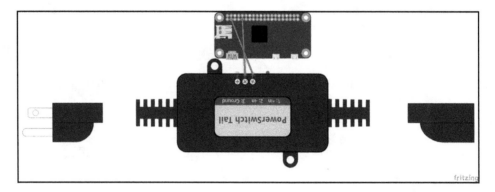

Raspberry Pi Zero interfaced to the PowerSwitch Tail II

The following is the LightSchedular class created:

```
class LightScheduler(object):
    """A Python class to turn on/off lights"""

    def __init__(self, start_time, stop_time):
        self.start_time = start_time
        self.stop_time = stop_time
        # lamp is connected to GPIO pin2.
        self.lights = OutputDevice(2)
```

Whenever an instance of LightScheduler is created, the GPIO pin is initialized to control the PowerSwitch Tail II. Now, let's add methods to turn on/off lights:

```
def init_schedule(self):
        # set the schedule
        schedule.every().day.at(self.start_time).do(self.on)
        schedule.every().day.at(self.stop_time).do(self.off)

    def on(self):
        """turn on lights"""
        self.lights.on()

    def off(self):
        """turn off lights"""
        self.lights.off()
```

In the init_schedule() method, the start and stop times that were passed as arguments are used to initialize schedule to turn on/off the lights at the specified times.

Put it together, we have:

```
import schedule
import time
from gpiozero import OutputDevice

class LightScheduler(object):
    """A Python class to turn on/off lights"""

    def __init__(self, start_time, stop_time):
        self.start_time = start_time
        self.stop_time = stop_time
        # lamp is connected to GPIO pin2.
        self.lights = OutputDevice(2)

    def init_schedule(self):
        # set the schedule
        schedule.every().day.at(self.start_time).do(self.on)
```

```
            schedule.every().day.at(self.stop_time).do(self.off)

      def on(self):
          """turn on lights"""
          self.lights.on()

      def off(self):
          """turn off lights"""
          self.lights.off()


  if __name__ == "__main__":
      lamp = LightScheduler("18:30", "9:30")
      lamp.on()
      time.sleep(50)
      lamp.off()
      lamp.init_schedule()
      while True:
          schedule.run_pending()
          time.sleep(1)
```

In the preceding example, the lights are scheduled to be turned on at 6:30 p.m. and turned off at 9:30 a.m. Once the jobs are scheduled, the program enters an infinite loop where it awaits task execution. This example could be run as a daemon by executing the file at start-up (add a line called `light_scheduler.py` to `/etc/rc.local`). After scheduling the job, it will continue to run as a daemon in the background.

This is just a basic introduction to OOP and its applications (keeping the beginner in mind). Refer to this book's website for more examples on OOP.

# Summary

In this chapter, we discussed lists and the advantages of OOP. We discussed OOP examples using the Raspberry Pi as the center of the examples. Since the book is targeted mostly towards beginners, we decided to stick to the basics of OOP while discussing examples. There are advanced aspects that are beyond the scope of the book. We leave it up to the reader to learn advanced concepts using other examples available on this book's site.

# 6
# File I/O and Python Utilities

In this chapter, we are going to discuss file I/O, that is reading, writing and appending to file in detail. We are also going to discuss Python utilities that enable manipulating files and interacting with the operating system. Each topic has a different level of complexity that we will discuss using an example. Let's get started!

## File I/O

We are discussing file I/O for two reasons:

- In the world of Linux operating systems, everything is a file. Interaction with peripherals on the Raspberry Pi is similar to reading from/writing to a file. For example: In Chapter 4, *Communication Interfaces*, we discussed serial port communication. You should be able to observe that serial port communication is like a file read/write operation.
- We use file I/O in some form in every project. For example: Writing sensor data to a CSV file or reading pre-configured options for a web server, and so on.

Hence, we thought it would be useful to discuss file I/O in Python as its own chapter (detailed documentation available from here: `https://docs.python.org/3/tutorial/inputoutput.html#reading-and-writing-files`) and discuss examples where it could play a role while developing applications on the Raspberry Pi Zero.

# Reading from a file

Let's create a simple text file, `read_file.txt` with the following text: `I am learning Python Programming using the Raspberry Pi Zero` and save it to the code samples directory (or any location of your choice).

To read from a file, we need to make use of the Python's in-built function: `open` to open the file. Let's take a quick look at a code snippet that demonstrates opening a text file to read its content and print it to the screen:

```python
if __name__ == "__main__":
    # open text file to read
    file = open('read_line.txt', 'r')
    # read from file and store it to data
    data = file.read()
    print(data)
    file.close()
```

Let's discuss this code snippet in detail:

1. The first step in reading the contents of the text file is opening the file using the in-built function `open`. The file in question needs to be passed as an argument along with a flag `r` that indicates we are opening the file to read the contents (We will discuss other flag options as we discuss each reading/writing files.)
2. Upon opening the file, the `open` function returns a pointer (address to the file object) that is stored in the `file` variable.

   ```python
   file = open('read_line.txt', 'r')
   ```

3. This file pointer is used to read the contents of the file and print it to the screen:

   ```python
   data = file.read()
   print(data)
   ```

4. After reading the contents of the file, the file is closed by calling the `close()` function.

Run the preceding code snippet (available for download along with this chapter—`read_from_file.py`) using IDLE3 or the command-line terminal. The contents of the text file would be printed to the screen as follows:

```
I am learning Python Programming using the Raspberry Pi Zero
```

# Reading lines

Sometimes, it is necessary to read the contents of a file by line-by-file. In Python, there are two options to do this: `readline()` and `readlines()`:

- `readline()`: As the name suggests, this in-built function enables reading one line at a time. Let's review this using an example:

```python
if __name__ == "__main__":
    # open text file to read
    file = open('read_line.txt', 'r')

    # read a line from the file
    data = file.readline()
    print(data)

    # read another line from the file
    data = file.readline()
    print(data)

    file.close()
```

When the preceding code snippet is executed (available for download as `read_line_from_file.py` along with this chapter), the `read_line.txt` file is opened and a single line is returned by the `readline()` function. This line is stored in the variable data. Since the function is called twice in this program, the output is as follows:

**I am learning Python Programming using the Raspberry Pi Zero.**

**This is the second line.**

A new line is returned every time the `readline` function is called and it returns an empty string when the end-of-file has reached.

- `readlines()`: This function reads the entire content of a file in lines and stores each it to a list:

```python
if __name__ == "__main__":
    # open text file to read
    file = open('read_lines.txt', 'r')

    # read a line from the file
    data = file.readlines()
    for line in data:
        print(line)
```

```
file.close()
```

Since the lines of the files is stored as a list, it could be retrieved by iterating through the list:

```
data = file.readlines()
     for line in data:
          print(line)
```

The preceding code snippet is available for download along with this chapter as read_lines_from_file.py.

# Writing to a file

Perform the following steps in order to write to a file:

1. The first step in writing to a file is opening a file with the write flag: w. If the file name that was passed as an argument doesn't exist, a new file is created:

```
file = open('write_file.txt', 'w')
```

2. Once the file is open, the next step is passing the string to be written as argument to the write() function:

```
file.write('I am excited to learn Python using
Raspberry Pi Zero')
```

3. Let's put the code together where we write a string to a text file, close it, re-open the file and print the contents of the file to the screen:

```
if __name__ == "__main__":
    # open text file to write
    file = open('write_file.txt', 'w')
    # write a line from the file
    file.write('I am excited to learn Python using
    Raspberry Pi Zero \n')
    file.close()

    file = open('write_file.txt', 'r')
    data = file.read()
    print(data)
    file.close()
```

4. The preceding code snippet is available for download along with this chapter (write_to_file.py).

5. When the preceding code snippet is executed, the output is shown as follows:

```
I am excited to learn Python using Raspberry Pi Zero
```

# Appending to a file

Whenever a file is opened using the write flag w, the contents of the file are deleted and opened afresh to write data. There is an alternative flag a that enables appending data to the end of the file. This flag also creates a new file if the file (that is passed as an argument to open) doesn't exist. Let's consider the code snippet below where we append a line to the text file write_file.txt from the previous section:

```
if __name__ == "__main__":
    # open text file to append
    file = open('write_file.txt', 'a')
    # append a line from the file
    file.write('This is a line appended to the file\n')
    file.close()

    file = open('write_file.txt', 'r')
    data = file.read()
    print(data)
    file.close()
```

When the preceding code snippet is executed (available for download along with this chapter—append_to_file.py), the string This is a line appended to the file is appended to the end of the text of the file. The contents of the file will include the following:

```
I am excited to learn Python using Raspberry Pi Zero
This is a line appended to the file
```

# seek

Once a file is opened, the file pointer that is used in file I/O moves from the beginning to the end of the file. It is possible to move the pointer to a specific position and read the data from that position. This is especially useful when we are interested in a specific line of a file. Let's consider the text file write_file.txt from the previous example. The contents of the file include:

```
I am excited to learn Python using Raspberry Pi Zero
This is a line appended to the file
```

Let's try to skip the first line and read only the second line using `seek`:

```python
if __name__ == "__main__":
    # open text file to read

    file = open('write_file.txt', 'r')

    # read the second line from the file
    file.seek(53)

    data = file.read()
    print(data)
    file.close()
```

In the preceding example (available for download along with this chapter as `seek_in_file.py`), the `seek` function is used to move the pointer to byte `53` that is the end of first line. Then the file's contents are read and stored into the variable. When this code snippet is executed, the output is as follows:

> **This is a line appended to the file**

Thus, seek enables moving the file pointer to a specific position.

## Read n bytes

The `seek` function enables moving the pointer to a specific position and reading a byte or n bytes from that position. Let's re-visit reading `write_file.txt` and try to read the word excited in the sentence `I am excited to learn Python using Raspberry Pi Zero`.

```python
if __name__ == "__main__":
    # open text file to read and write
    file = open('write_file.txt', 'r')

    # set the pointer to the desired position
    file.seek(5)
    data = file.read(1)
    print(data)

    # rewind the pointer
    file.seek(5)
    data = file.read(7)
    print(data)
    file.close()
```

The preceding code can be explained in the following steps:

1. In the first step, the file is opened using the `read` flag and the file pointer is set to the fifth byte (using `seek`)—the position of the letter `e` in the contents of the text file.

2. Now, we read one byte from the file by passing it as an argument to the `read` function. When an integer is passed as an argument, the `read` function returns the corresponding number of bytes from the file. When no argument is passed, it reads the entire file. The `read` function returns an empty string if the file is empty:

```
file.seek(5)
data = file.read(1)
print(data)
```

3. In the second part, we try to read the word `excited` from the text file. We rewind the position of the pointer back to the fifth byte. Then we read seven bytes from the file (length of the word `excited`).

4. When the code snippet is executed (available for download along with this chapter as `seek_to_read.py`), the program should print the letter `e` and the word `excited`:

```
file.seek(5)
data = file.read(7)
print(data)
```

# r+

We discussed reading and writing to files using the `r` and `w` flags. There is another called `r+`. This flag enables reading and writing to a file. Let's review an example that enables us to understand this flag.

Let's review the contents of `write_file.txt` once again:

```
I am excited to learn Python using Raspberry Pi Zero
This is a line appended to the file
```

Let's modify the second line to read: `This is a line that was modified`. The code sample is available for download along with this chapter as `seek_to_write.py`.

```
if __name__ == "__main__":
    # open text file to read and write
    file = open('write_file.txt', 'r+')
```

```
# set the pointer to the desired position
file.seek(68)
file.write('that was modified \n')

# rewind the pointer to the beginning of the file
file.seek(0)
data = file.read()
print(data)
file.close()
```

Let's review how this example works:

1. The first step in this example is opening the file using the r+ flag. This enables reading and writing to the file.
2. The next step is moving to the 68th byte of the file
3. The that was modified string is written to the file at this position. The spaces at the end of the string are used to overwrite the original content of the second sentence.
4. Now, the file pointer is set to the beginning of the file and its contents are read.
5. When the preceding code snippet is executed, the modified file contents are printed to the screen as follows:

```
I am excited to learn Python using Raspberry Pi Zero
This is a line that was modified
```

There is another a+ flag that enables appending data to the end of the file and reading at the same time. We will leave this to the reader to figure out using the examples discussed so far.

 We have discussed different examples on reading and writing to files in Python. It can be overwhelming without sufficient experience in programming. We strongly recommend working through the different code samples provided in this chapter

## Challenge to the reader

Use the a+ flag to open the write_file.txt file (discussed in different examples) and append a line to the file. Set the file pointer using seek and print its contents. You may open the file only once in the program.

# The with keyword

So far, we discussed different flags that could be used to open files in different modes. The examples we discussed followed a common pattern—open the file, perform read/write operations and close the file. There is an elegant way of interacting with files using the `with` keyword.

If there are any errors during the execution of the code block that interacts with a file, the `with` keyword ensures that the file is closed and the associated resources are cleaned up on exiting the code block. As always, let's review the `with` keyword with an example:

```
if __name__ == "__main__":
    with open('write_file.txt', 'r+') as file:
            # read the contents of the file and print to the screen
            print(file.read())
            file.write("This is a line appended to the file")

            #rewind the file and read its contents
            file.seek(0)
            print(file.read())
    # the file is automatically closed at this point
    print("Exited the with keyword code block")
```

In the preceding example (`with_keyword_example`), we skipped closing the file as the `with` keyword takes care of closing the file once the execution of the indented code block is complete. The `with` keyword also takes care of closing the file while leaving the code block due to an error. This ensures that the resources are cleaned up properly in any scenario. Going forward, we will be using the `with` keyword for file I/O.

# configparser

Let's discuss some aspects of Python programming that is especially helpful while developing applications using the Raspberry Pi. One such tool is the `configparser` available in Python. The `configparser` module (`https://docs.python.org/3.4/library/configparser.html`) is used to read/write config files for applications.

In software development, config files are generally used to store constants such as access credentials, device ID, and so on In the context of a Raspberry Pi, `configparser` could be used to store the list of all GPIO pins in use, addresses of sensors interfaced via the I²C interface, and so on. Let's discuss three examples where we learn making use of the `configparser` module. In the first example we will create a `config` file using the `configparser`.

In the second example, we will make use of the `configparser` to read the config values and in the third example, we will discuss modifying config files in the final example.

**Example 1**:

In the first example, let's create a config file that stores information including device ID, GPIO pins in use, sensor interface address, debug switch, and access credentials:

```
import configparser

if __name__ == "__main__":
    # initialize ConfigParser
    config_parser = configparser.ConfigParser()

    # Let's create a config file
    with open('raspi.cfg', 'w') as config_file:
            #Let's add a section called ApplicationInfo
            config_parser.add_section('AppInfo')

            #let's add config information under this section
            config_parser.set('AppInfo', 'id', '123')
            config_parser.set('AppInfo', 'gpio', '2')
            config_parser.set('AppInfo', 'debug_switch', 'True')
            config_parser.set('AppInfo', 'sensor_address', '0x62')

            #Let's add another section for credentials
            config_parser.add_section('Credentials')
            config_parser.set('Credentials', 'token', 'abcxyz123')
            config_parser.write(config_file)
    print("Config File Creation Complete")
```

Let's discuss the preceding code example (available for download along with this chapter as `config_parser_write.py`) in detail:

1. The first step is importing the `configparser` module and creating an instance of the `ConfigParser` class. This instance is going to be called `config_parser`:

   ```
   config_parser = configparser.ConfigParser()
   ```

2. Now, we open a config file called `raspi.cfg` using the `with` keyword. Since the file doesn't exist, a new config file is created.
3. The config file is going to consist of two sections namely `AppInfo` and `Credentials`.

4. The two sections could be created using the `add_section` method as follows:

```
config_parser.add_section('AppInfo')
config_parser.add_section('Credentials')
```

5. Each section is going to consist of different set of constants. Each constant could be added to the relevant section using the `set` method. The required arguments to the `set` method include the section name (under which the parameter/constant is going to be located), the name of the parameter/constant and its corresponding value. For example: The `id` parameter can be added to the `AppInfo` section and assigned a value of `123` as follows:

```
config_parser.set('AppInfo', 'id', '123')
```

6. The final step is saving these config values to the file. This is accomplished using the `config_parser` method, `write`. The file is closed once the program exits the indented block under the `with` keyword:

```
config_parser.write(config_file)
```

 We strongly recommend trying the code snippets yourself and use these snippets as a reference. You will learn a lot by making mistakes and possibly arrive with a better solution than the one discussed here.

When the preceding code snippet is executed, a config file called `raspi.cfg` is created. The contents of the config file would include the contents shown as follows:

```
[AppInfo]
id = 123
gpio = 2
debug_switch = True
sensor_address = 0x62

[Credentials]
token = abcxyz123
```

**Example 2**:

Let's discuss an example where we read config parameters from a config file created in the previous example:

```
import configparser

if __name__ == "__main__":
    # initialize ConfigParser
```

```
config_parser = configparser.ConfigParser()

# Let's read the config file
config_parser.read('raspi.cfg')

# Read config variables
device_id = config_parser.get('AppInfo', 'id')
debug_switch = config_parser.get('AppInfo', 'debug_switch')
sensor_address = config_parser.get('AppInfo', 'sensor_address')

# execute the code if the debug switch is true
if debug_switch == "True":
        print("The device id is " + device_id)
        print("The sensor_address is " + sensor_address)
```

 If the config files are created in the format shown, the `ConfigParser` class should be able to parse it. It is not really necessary to create config files using a Python program. We just wanted to show programmatic creation of config files as it is easier to programmatically create config files for multiple devices at the same time.

The preceding example is available for download along with this chapter (`config_parser_read.py`). Let's discuss how this code sample works:

1. The first step is initializing an instance of the `ConfigParser` class called `config_parser`.

2. The second step is loading and reading the config file using the instance method `read`.

3. Since we know the structure of the config file, let's go ahead and read some constants available under the section `AppInfo`. The config file parameters can be read using the `get` method. The required arguments include the section under which the config parameter is located and the name of the parameter. For example: The config `id` parameter is located under the `AppInfo` section. Hence, the required arguments to the method include `AppInfo` and `id`:

   ```
   device_id = config_parser.get('AppInfo', 'id')
   ```

4. Now that the config parameters are read into variables, let's make use of it in our program. For example: Let's test if the `debug_switch` variable (a switch to determine if the program is in debug mode) and print the other config parameters that were retrieved from the file:

```
if debug_switch == "True":
    print("The device id is " + device_id)
    print("The sensor_address is " + sensor_address)
```

**Example 3:**

Let's discuss an example where we would like to modify an existing config file. This is especially useful in situations where we need to update the firmware version number in the config file after performing a firmware update.

The following code snippet is available for download as `config_parser_modify.py` along with this chapter:

```
import configparser

if __name__ == "__main__":
    # initialize ConfigParser
    config_parser = configparser.ConfigParser()

    # Let's read the config file
    config_parser.read('raspi.cfg')

    # Set firmware version
    config_parser.set('AppInfo', 'fw_version', 'A3')

    # write the updated config to the config file
    with open('raspi.cfg', 'w') as config_file:
        config_parser.write(config_file)
```

Let's discuss how this works:

1. As always, the first step is initializing an instance of the `ConfigParser` class. The config file is loaded using the method `read`:

```
# initialize ConfigParser
config_parser = configparser.ConfigParser()

# Let's read the config file
config_parser.read('raspi.cfg')
```

2. The required parameter is updated using the `set` method (discussed in a previous example):

```
# Set firmware version
config_parser.set('AppInfo', 'fw_version', 'A3')
```

3. The updated config is saved to the config file using the `write` method:

```
with open('raspi.cfg', 'w') as config_file:
    config_parser.write(config_file)
```

## Challenge to the reader

Using example 3 as a reference, update the config parameter `debug_switch` to the value `False`. Repeat example 2 and see what happens.

# Reading/writing to CSV files

In this section, we are going to discuss reading/writing to CSV files. This module (`https://docs.python.org/3.4/library/csv.html`) is useful in data logging applications. Since we will be discussing data logging in the next chapter, let's review reading/writing to CSV files.

# Writing to CSV files

Let's consider a scenario where we are reading data from different sensors. This data needs to be recorded to a CSV file where each column corresponds to a reading from a specific sensor. We are going to discuss an example where we record the value `123`, `456`, and `789` in the first row of the CSV file and the second row is going to consist of values including `Red`, `Green`, and `Blue`:

1. The first step in writing to a CSV file is opening a CSV file using the `with` keyword:

```
with open("csv_example.csv", 'w') as csv_file:
```

2. The next step is initializing an instance of the `writer` class of the CSV module:

```
csv_writer = csv.writer(csv_file)
```

3. Now, each row is added to the file by creating a list that contains all the elements that need to be added to a row. For example: The first row can be added to the list as follows:

```
csv_writer.writerow([123, 456, 789])
```

4. Putting it altogether, we have:

```
import csv
if __name__ == "__main__":
    # initialize csv writer
    with open("csv_example.csv", 'w') as csv_file:
        csv_writer = csv.writer(csv_file)
        csv_writer.writerow([123, 456, 789])
        csv_writer.writerow(["Red", "Green", "Blue"])
```

5. When the above code snippet is executed (available for download as `csv_write.py` along with this chapter), a CSV file is created in the local directory with the following contents:

```
123,456,789
Red,Green,Blue
```

# Reading from CSV files

Let's discuss an example where we read the contents of the CSV file created in the previous section:

1. The first step in reading a CSV file is opening it in read mode:

```
with open("csv_example.csv", 'r') as csv_file:
```

2. Next, we initialize an instance of the `reader` class from the CSV module. The contents of the CSV file are loaded into the object `csv_reader`:

```
csv_reader = csv.reader(csv_file)
```

3. Now that the contents of the CSV file are loaded, each row of the CSV file could be retrieved as follows:

```
for row in csv_reader:
    print(row)
```

4. Put it all together:

```python
import csv

if __name__ == "__main__":
    # initialize csv writer
    with open("csv_example.csv", 'r') as csv_file:
        csv_reader = csv.reader(csv_file)

        for row in csv_reader:
            print(row)
```

5. When the preceding code snippet is executed (available for download along with this chapter as `csv_read.py`), the contents of the file are printed row-by-row where each row is a list that contains the comma separated values:

```
['123', '456', '789']
['Red', 'Green', 'Blue']
```

# Python utilities

Python comes with several utilities that enables interacting with other files and the operating system itself. We have identified all those Python utilities that we have used in our past projects. Let's discuss the different modules and their uses as we might use them in the final project of this book.

# The os module

As the name suggests, this module (`https://docs.python.org/3.1/library/os.html`) enables interacting with the operating system. Let's discuss some of its applications with examples.

# Checking a file's existence

The `os` module could be used to check if a file exists in a specific directory. For example: We extensively made use of the `write_file.txt` file. Before opening this file to read or write, we could check the file's existence:

```python
import os
if __name__ == "__main__":
    # Check if file exists
```

```
if os.path.isfile('/home/pi/Desktop/code_samples/write_file.txt'):
    print('The file exists!')
else:
    print('The file does not exist!')
```

In the preceding code snippet, we make use of the isfile() function, available with the os.path module. When a file's location is passed an argument to the function, it returns True if the file exists at that location. In this example, since the file write_file.txt exists in the code examples directory, the function returns True. Hence the message, The file exists is printed to the screen:

```
if os.path.isfile('/home/pi/Desktop/code_samples/write_file.txt'):
    print('The file exists!')
else:
    print('The file does not exist!')
```

# Checking for a folder's existence

Similar to os.path.isfile(), there is another function called os.path.isdir(). It returns True if a folder exists at a specific location. We have been reviewing all code samples from a folder called code_samples located on the Raspberry Pi's desktop. It's existence could be confirmed as follows:

```
# Confirm code_samples' existence
if os.path.isdir('/home/pi/Desktop/code_samples'):
    print('The directory exists!')
else:
    print('The directory does not exist!')
```

# Deleting files

The os module also enables deleting files using the remove() function. Any file that is passed as an argument to the function is deleted. In the *File I/O* section, we discussed reading from files using the text file, read_file.txt. Let's delete the file by passing it as an argument to the remove() function:

```
os.remove('/home/pi/Desktop/code_samples/read_file.txt')
```

# Killing a process

It is possible to kill an application running on the Raspberry Pi by passing process `pid` to the `kill()` function. In the previous chapter, we discussed the `light_scheduler` example that runs as a background process on the Raspberry Pi. To demonstrate killing a process, we are going to attempt killing that process. We need to determine the process `pid` of the `light_scheduler` process (you may pick an application that was started by you as a user and not do not touch root processes). The process `pid` could be retrieved from the command-line terminal using the following command:

```
ps aux
```

It spits out the processes currently running on the Raspberry Pi (shown in the following figure). The process `pid` for the `light_scheduler` application is **1815**:

```
pi        822  0.0  1.1   6916  5000 pts/0    Ss   Jul10   0:02 -bash
root      1548  0.0  0.0      0     0 ?        S    Jul10   0:00 [kworker/u2:1]
pi        1815  0.1  1.9  12636  8804 pts/0    S+   Jul10   0:01 python3 light_scheduler.py
root      1817  0.0  1.1  12064  5280 ?        Ss   Jul10   0:00 sshd: pi [priv]
pi        1827  0.0  0.7  12064  3504 ?        S    Jul10   0:00 sshd: pi@pts/1
pi        1830  0.0  1.0   6320  4476 pts/1    Ss   Jul10   0:00 -bash
```

light_scheduler daemon's PID

Assuming we know the process `pid` of the application that needs to be killed, let's review killing the function using `kill()`. The arguments required to kill the function include the process `pid` and signal (`signal.SIGKILL`) that needs to be sent to the process to kill the application:

```python
import os
import signal
if __name__ == "__main__":
    #kill the application
    try:
        os.kill(1815, signal.SIGKILL)
    except OSError as error:
        print("OS Error " + str(error))
```

The `signal` module (https://docs.python.org/3/library/signal.html) contains the constants that represents the signals that could be used to stop an application. In this code snippet, we make use of the `SIGKILL` signal. Try running the `ps` command (`ps aux`) and you will notice that the `light_scheduler` application has been killed.

# Monitoring a process

In the previous example, we discussed killing an application using the `kill()` function. You might have noticed that we made use of something called the `try`/`except` keywords to attempt killing the application. We will discuss these keywords in detail in the next chapter.

It is also possible to monitor whether an application is running using the `kill()` function using the `try`/`except` keywords. We will discuss monitoring processes using the `kill()` function after introducing the concept of trapping exceptions using `try`/`except` keywords.

All examples discussed in the `os` module are available for download along with this chapter as `os_utils.py`.

# The glob module

The `glob` module (`https://docs.python.org/3/library/glob.html`) enables identifying files of a specific extension or files that have a specific pattern. For example, it is possible to list all Python files in a folder as follows:

```
# List all files
for file in glob.glob('*.py'):
    print(file)
```

The `glob()` function returns a list of files that contains the `.py` extension. A `for` loop is used to iterate through the list and print each file. When the preceding code snippet is executed, the output contains the list of all code samples belonging to this chapter (output truncated for representation):

```
read_from_file.py
config_parser_read.py
append_to_file.py
read_line_from_file.py
config_parser_modify.py
python_utils.py
config_parser_write.py
csv_write.py
```

This module is especially helpful with listing files that have a specific pattern. For example: Let's consider a scenario where you would like to upload files that were created from different trials of an experiment. You are only interested in files that are of the following format: `file1xx.txt` where x stands for any digit between 0 and 9. Those files could be sorted and listed as follows:

```
# List all files of the format 1xx.txt
for file in glob.glob('txt_files/file1[0-9][0-9].txt'):
    print(file)
```

In the preceding example, `[0-9]` means that the file name could contain any digit between 0 and 9. Since we are looking for files of the `file1xx.txt` format, the search pattern that is passed an argument to the `glob()` function is `file1[0-9][0-9].txt`.

When the preceding code snippet is executed, the output contains all text files of the specified format:

```
txt_files/file126.txt
txt_files/file125.txt
txt_files/file124.txt
txt_files/file123.txt
txt_files/file127.txt
```

We came across this article that explains the use of expressions for sorting files: `http://www.linuxjournal.com/content/bash-extended-globbing`. The same concept can be extended to searching for files using the `glob` module.

## Challenge to the reader

The examples discussed with the `glob` module are available for download along with this chapter as `glob_example.py`. In one of the examples, we discussed listing files of a specific format. How would you go about listing files that are of the following format: `filexxxx.*`? (Here x represents any number between 0 and 9. * represents any file extension.)

# The shutil module

The `shutil` module (`https://docs.python.org/3/library/shutil.html`) enables moving and copying files between folders using the `move()` and `copy()` methods. In the previous section, we listed all text files within the folder, `txt_files`. Let's move these files to the current directory (where the code is being executed) using `move()`, make a copy of these files once again in `txt_files` and finally remove the text files from the current directory:

```
import glob
import shutil
import os
if __name__ == "__main__":
    # move files to the current directory
    for file in glob.glob('txt_files/file1[0-9][0-9].txt'):
        shutil.move(file, '.')
    # make a copy of files in the folder 'txt_files' and delete them
    for file in glob.glob('file1[0-9][0-9].txt'):
        shutil.copy(file, 'txt_files')
        os.remove(file)
```

In the preceding example (available for download along with this chapter as `shutil_example.py`), the files are being moved as well as copied from the origin to the destination by specifying the source and the destination as the first and second arguments respectively.

The files to be moved (or copied) are identified using the `glob` module. Then, each file is moved or copied using their corresponding methods.

# The subprocess module

We briefly discussed this module in the previous chapter. The `subprocess` module (`https://docs.python.org/3.2/library/subprocess.html`) enables launching another program from within a Python program. One of the commonly used functions from the `subprocess` module is `Popen`. Any process that needs to be launched from within the program needs to be passed as a list argument to the `Popen` function:

```
import subprocess
if __name__ == "__main__":
    subprocess.Popen(['aplay', 'tone.wav'])
```

In the preceding example, `tone.wav` (WAVE file that needs to be played) and the command that needs to be run are passed as a list argument to the function. There are several other commands from the `subprocess` module that serve a similar purpose. We leave it to your exploration.

# The sys module

The `sys` module (`https://docs.python.org/3/library/sys.html`) allows interacting with the Python run-time interpreter. One of the functions of the `sys` module is parsing command-line arguments provided as inputs to the program. Let's write a program that reads and prints the contents of the file that is passed as an argument to the program:

```
import sys
if __name__ == "__main__":
    with open(sys.argv[1], 'r') as read_file:
        print(read_file.read())
```

Try running the preceding example as follows:

**python3 sys_example.py read_lines.txt**

The preceding example is available for download along with this chapter as `sys_example.py`. The list of command-line arguments passed while running the program are available as a `argv` list in the `sys` module. `argv[0]` is usually the name of the Python program and `argv[1]` is usually the first argument passed to the function.

When `sys_example.py` is executed with `read_lines.txt` as an argument, the program should print the contents of the text file:

```
I am learning Python Programming using the Raspberry Pi Zero.
This is the second line.
Line 3.
Line 4.
Line 5.
Line 6.
Line 7.
```

# Summary

In this chapter, we discussed file I/O – reading and writing to files, different flags used to read, write, and append to files. We talked about moving file pointers to different points in a file to retrieve specific content or overwrite the contents of a file at a specific location. We discussed the `ConfigParser` module in Python and its application in storing/retrieving config parameters for applications along with reading and writing to CSV files.

Finally, we discussed different Python utilities that have a potential use in our project. We will be extensively making use of file I/O and the discussed Python utilities in our final project. We strongly recommend familiarizing yourself with the concepts discussed in this chapter before moving onto the final projects discussed in this book.

In the upcoming chapters, we will discuss uploading sensor data stored in CSV files to the cloud and logging errors encountered during the execution of an application. See you in the next chapter!

# 7
# Requests and Web Frameworks

The main topics of this chapter are requests and web frameworks in Python. We are going to discuss libraries and frameworks that enable retrieving data from the Web (for example, get weather updates), upload data to a remote server (for example, log sensor data), or control appliances on a local network. We will also discuss topics that will help with learning the core topics of this chapter.

## The try/except keywords

So far, we have reviewed and tested all our examples assuming the ideal condition, that is, the execution of the program will encounter no errors. On the contrary, applications fail from time to time either due to external factors, such as invalid user input and poor Internet connectivity, or program logic errors caused by the programmer. In such cases, we want the program to report/log the nature of error and either continue its execution or clean up resources before exiting the program. The try/except keywords offer a mechanism to trap an error that occurs during a program's execution and take remedial action. Because it is possible to trap and log an error in crucial parts of the code, the try/except keywords are especially useful while debugging an application.

Let's understand the try/except keywords by comparing two examples. Let's build a simple guessing game where the user is asked to guess a number between 0 and 9:

1. A random number (between 0 and 9) is generated using Python's random module. If the user's guess of the generated number is right, the Python program declares the user as the winner and exits the game.
2. If the user input is the letter x, the program quits the game.

3. The user input is converted into an integer using the `int()` function. A sanity check is performed to determine whether the user input is a number between 0 and 9.

4. The integer is compared against a random number. If they are the same, the user is declared the winner and the program exits the game.

Let's observe what happens when we deliberately provide an erroneous input to this program (the code snippet shown here is available for download along with this chapter as `guessing_game.py`):

```python
import random

if __name__ == "__main__":
    while True:
        # generate a random number between 0 and 9
        rand_num = random.randrange(0,10)

        # prompt the user for a number
        value = input("Enter a number between 0 and 9: ")

        if value == 'x':
            print("Thanks for playing! Bye!")
            break

        input_value = int(value)

        if input_value < 0 or input_value > 9:
            print("Input invalid. Enter a number between 0 and 9.")


        if input_value == rand_num:
            print("Your guess is correct! You win!")
            break
        else:
            print("Nope! The random value was %s" % rand_num)
```

Let's execute the preceding code snippet and provide the input `hello` to the program:

```
Enter a number between 0 and 9: hello
Traceback (most recent call last):
    File "guessing_game.py", line 12, in <module>
        input_value = int(value)
ValueError: invalid literal for int() with base 10: 'hello'
```

In the preceding example, the program fails when it is trying to convert the user input `hello` to an integer. The program execution ends with an exception. An exception highlights the line where the error has occurred. In this case, it has occurred in line 10:

```
File "guessing_game.py", line 12, in <module>
input_value = int(value)
```

The nature of the error is also highlighted in the exception. In this example, the last line indicates that the exception thrown is `ValueError`:

```
ValueError: invalid literal for int() with base 10: 'hello'
```

Let's discuss the same example (available for download along with this chapter as `try_and_except.py`) that makes use of the `try`/`except` keywords. It is possible to continue playing the game after trapping this exception and printing it to the screen. We have the following code:

```python
import random

if __name__ == "__main__":
    while True:
        # generate a random number between 0 and 9
        rand_num = random.randrange(0,10)

        # prompt the user for a number
        value = input("Enter a number between 0 and 9: ")

        if value == 'x':
            print("Thanks for playing! Bye!")

        try:
            input_value = int(value)
        except ValueError as error:
            print("The value is invalid %s" % error)
            continue

        if input_value < 0 or input_value > 9:
            print("Input invalid. Enter a number between 0 and 9.")
            continue

        if input_value == rand_num:
            print("Your guess is correct! You win!")
            break
        else:
            print("Nope! The random value was %s" % rand_num)
```

Let's discuss how the same example works with the try/except keywords:

1.  From the previous example, we know that when a user provides the wrong input (for example, a letter instead of a number between 0 and 9), the exception occurs at line 10 (where the user input is converted into an integer), and the nature of the error is named ValueError.

2.  It is possible to avoid interruption of the program's execution by wrapping this in a try...except block:

    ```
    try:
        input_value = int(value)
    except ValueError as error:
        print("The value is invalid %s" % error)
    ```

3.  On receiving a user input, the program attempts converting the user input into an integer under the try block.

4.  If ValueError has occurred, error is trapped by the except block, and the following message is printed to the screen along with the actual error message:

    ```
    except ValueError as error:
        print("The value is invalid %s" % error)
    ```

5.  Try executing the code example and try providing an invalid input. You will note that the program prints the error message (along with the nature of the error) and goes back to the top of the game loop and continues seeking valid user input:

    ```
    Enter a number between 0 and 9: 3
    Nope! The random value was 5
    Enter a number between 0 and 9: hello
    The value is invalid invalid literal for int() with
    base 10: 'hello'
    Enter a number between 0 and 10: 4
    Nope! The random value was 6
    ```

The try...except block comes with a substantial processing power cost. Hence, it is important to keep the try...except block as short as possible. Because we know that the error occurs on the line where we attempt converting the user input into an integer, we wrap it in a try...except block to trap an error.

Thus, the try/except keywords are used to prevent any abnormal behavior in a program's execution due to an error. It enables logging the error and taking remedial action. Similar to the try...except block, there are also try...except...else and try...except...else code blocks. Let's quickly review those options with a couple of examples.

# try...except...else

The `try...except...else` block is especially useful when we want a certain block of code to be executed only when no exceptions are raised. In order to demonstrate this concept, let's rewrite the guessing game example using this block:

```
try:
    input_value = int(value)
except ValueError as error:
    print("The value is invalid %s" % error)
else:
    if input_value < 0 or input_value > 9:
        print("Input invalid. Enter a number between 0 and 9.")
    elif input_value == rand_num:
        print("Your guess is correct! You win!")
        break
    else:
        print("Nope! The random value was %s" % rand_num)
```

The modified guessing game example that makes use of the `try...except...else` block is available for download along with this chapter as `try_except_else.py`. In this example, the program compares the user input against the random number only if a valid user input was received. It otherwise skips the `else` block and goes back to the top of the loop to accept the next user input. Thus, `try...except...else` is used when we want a specific code block to be executed when no exceptions are raised due to the code in the `try` block.

# try...except...else...finally

As the name suggests, the `finally` block is used to execute a block of code on leaving the `try` block. This block of code is executed even after an exception is raised. This is useful in scenarios where we need to clean up resources and free up memory before moving on to the next stage.

Let's demonstrate the function of the `finally` block using our guessing game. To understand how the `finally` keyword works, let's make use of a counter variable named `count` that is incremented in the `finally` block, and another counter variable named `valid_count` that is incremented in the `else` block. We have the following code:

```
count = 0
valid_count = 0
while True:
    # generate a random number between 0 and 9
```

```
rand_num = random.randrange(0,10)

# prompt the user for a number
value = input("Enter a number between 0 and 9: ")

if value == 'x':
    print("Thanks for playing! Bye!")

try:
    input_value = int(value)
except ValueError as error:
    print("The value is invalid %s" % error)
else:
    if input_value < 0 or input_value > 9:
        print("Input invalid. Enter a number between 0 and 9.")
        continue

    valid_count += 1
    if input_value == rand_num:
        print("Your guess is correct! You win!")
        break
    else:
        print("Nope! The random value was %s" % rand_num)
finally:
    count += 1

print("You won the game in %d attempts "\
    "and %d inputs were valid" % (count, valid_count))
```

The preceding code snippet is from the `try_except_else_finally.py` code
sample (available for download along with this chapter). Try executing the code sample and
playing the game. You will note the total number of attempts it took to win the game and
the number of inputs that were valid:

```
Enter a number between 0 and 9: g
The value is invalid invalid literal for int() with
base 10: 'g'
Enter a number between 0 and 9: 3
Your guess is correct! You win!
You won the game in 9 attempts and 8 inputs were valid
```

This demonstrates how the `try-except-else-finally` block works. Any code under the
`else` keyword is executed when the critical code block (under the `try` keyword) is
executed successfully, whereas the code block under the `finally` keyword is executed
while exiting the `try...except` block (useful for cleaning up resources while exiting a
code block).

Try providing invalid inputs while playing the game using the previous code example to understand the code block flow.

# Connecting to the Internet – web requests

Now that we discussed the `try/except` keywords, let's make use of it to build a simple application that connects to the Internet. We will write a simple application that retrieves the current time from the Internet. We will be making use of the `requests` library for Python (`http://requests.readthedocs.io/en/master/#`).

The `requests` module enables connecting to the Web and retrieving information. In order to do so, we need to make use of the `get()` method from the `requests` module to make a request:

```
import requests
response = requests.get('http://nist.time.gov/actualtime.cgi')
```

In the preceding code snippet, we are passing a URL as an argument to the `get()` method. In this case, it is the URL that returns the current time in the Unix format (`https://en.wikipedia.org/wiki/Unix_time`).

Let's make use of the `try/except` keywords to make a request to get the current time:

```
#!/usr/bin/python3

import requests

if __name__ == "__main__":
    # Source for link: http://stackoverflow.com/a/30635751/822170
    try:
        response = requests.get('http://nist.time.gov/actualtime.cgi')
        print(response.text)
    except requests.exceptions.ConnectionError as error:
        print("Something went wrong. Try again")
```

In the preceding example (available for download along with this chapter as `internet_access.py`), the request is made under the `try` block, and the response (returned by `response.text`) is printed to the screen.

If there is an error while executing the request to retrieve the current time, `ConnectionError` is raised (http://requests.readthedocs.io/en/master/user/quickstart/#errors-and-exceptions). This error could either be caused by the lack of an Internet connection or an incorrect URL. This error is caught by the `except` block. Try running the example, and it should return the current time from `time.gov`:

```
<timestamp time="1474421525322329" delay="0"/>
```

# The application of requests – retrieving weather information

Let's make use of the `requests` module to retrieve the weather information for the city of San Francisco. We will be making use of the **OpenWeatherMap** API (`openweathermap.org`) to retrieve the weather information:

1. In order to make use of the API, sign up for an API account and get an API key (it is free of charge):

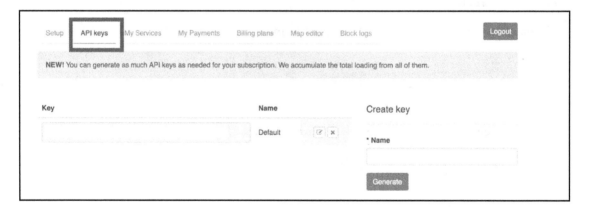

An API key from openweathermap.org

2. According to the API documentation (`openweathermap.org/current`), the weather information for a city can be retrieved using `http://api.openweathermap.org/data/2.5/weather?zip=SanFrancisco&appid=API_KEY&units=imperial` as the URL.

3. Substitute API_KEY with the key from your account and use it to retrieve the current weather information in a browser. You should be able to retrieve the weather information in the following format:

```
{"coord":{"lon":-122.42,"lat":37.77},"weather":[{"id":800,
"main":"Clear","description":"clear sky","icon":"01n"}],"base":
"stations","main":{"temp":71.82,"pressure":1011,"humidity":50,
"temp_min":68,"temp_max":75.99},"wind":{"speed":13.04,"deg":291},
"clouds":{"all":0},"dt":1474505391,"sys":{"type":3,"id":9966,
"message":0.0143,"country":"US","sunrise":1474552682,
"sunset":1474596336},"id":5391959,"name":"San Francisco","cod":200}
```

The weather information (shown previously) is returned in the JSON format. **JavaScript Object Notation (JSON)** is a data format that is widely used to exchange data over the Web. The main advantage of JSON format is that it is in a readable format and many popular programming languages support encapsulating data in JSON format. As shown in the earlier snippet, JSON format enables exchanging information in readable name/value pairs.

Let's review retrieving the weather using the `requests` module and parsing the JSON data:

1. Substitute the URL in the previous example (`internet_access.py`) with the one discussed in this example. This should return the weather information in the JSON format.

2. The requests module provides a method to parse the JSON data. The response could be parsed as follows:

```
response = requests.get(URL)
json_data = response.json()
```

3. The `json()` function parses the response from the OpenWeatherMap API and returns a dictionary of different weather parameters (`json_data`) and their values.

4. Since we know the response format from the API documentation, the current temperature could be retrieved from the parsed response as follows:

```
print(json_data['main']['temp'])
```

5. Putting it all together, we have this:

```
#!/usr/bin/python3

import requests
```

```
# generate your own API key
APP_ID = '5d6f02fd4472611a20f4ce602010ee0c'
ZIP = 94103
URL = """http://api.openweathermap.org/data/2.5/weather?zip={}
&appid={}&units=imperial""".format(ZIP, APP_ID)

if __name__ == "__main__":
    # API Documentation: http://openweathermap.org/
    current#current_JSON
    try:
        # encode data payload and post it
        response = requests.get(URL)
        json_data = response.json()
        print("Temperature is %s degrees Fahrenheit" %
        json_data['main']['temp'])
    except requests.exceptions.ConnectionError as error:
        print("The error is %s" % error)
```

The preceding example is available for download along with this chapter as
`weather_example.py`. The example should display the current temperature as follows:

```
Temperature is 68.79 degrees Fahrenheit
```

# The application of requests – publishing events to the Internet

In the previous example, we retrieved information from the Internet. Let's consider an example where we have to publish a sensor event somewhere on the Internet. This could be either a cat door opening while you are away from home or someone at your doorstep stepping on the doormat. Because we discussed interfacing sensors to the Raspberry Pi Zero in the previous chapter, let's discuss a scenario where we could post these events to *Slack*—a workplace communication tool, Twitter, or cloud services such as **Phant** (`https://data.sp arkfun.com/`).

In this example, we will post these events to Slack using `requests`. Let's send a direct message to ourselves on Slack whenever a sensor event such as a cat door opening occurs. We need a URL to post these sensor events to Slack. Let's review generating a URL in order to post sensor events to Slack:

1. The first step in generating a URL is creating an *incoming webhook*. A webhook is a type request that can post messages that are carried as a payload to applications such as Slack.

2. If you are a member of a Slack team named *TeamX*, launch your team's application directory, namely `teamx.slack.com/apps` in a browser:

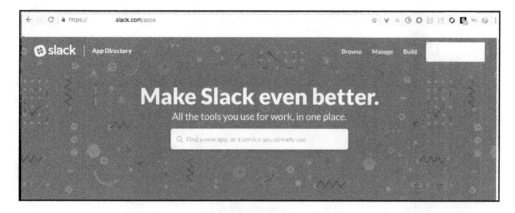

Launch your team's app directory

3. Search for `incoming webhooks` in your app directory and select the first option, **Incoming WebHooks** (as shown in the following screenshot):

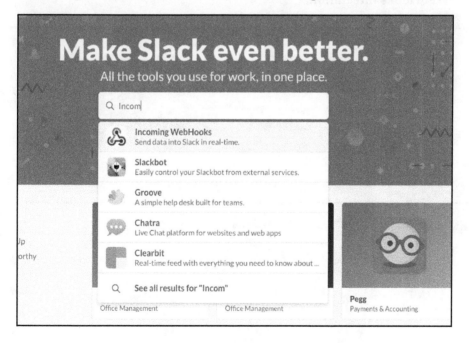

Select incoming webhooks

4. Click on **Add Configuration**:

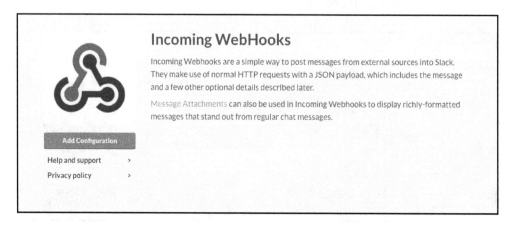

Add Configuration

5. Let's send a private message to ourselves when an event occurs. Select **Privately to (you)** as the option and create a webhook by clicking on **Add Incoming WebHooks integration**:

Select Privately to you

6. We have generated a URL to send direct messages about sensor events (URL partially concealed):

| Webhook URL | `https://hooks.slack.com/services/` |
|---|---|
| Sending Messages | You have two options for sending data to the Webhook URL above:<br>• Send a JSON string as the `payload` parameter in a POST request<br>• Send a JSON string as the body of a POST request<br><br>For a simple message, your JSON payload could contain a `text` property at minimum. This is the text that will be posted to the channel.<br>A simple example:<br><br>`payload={"text": "This is a line of text in a channel.\nAnd this is` |

Generated URL

7. Now, we can send direct message to ourselves on Slack using the previously-mentioned URL. The sensor event can be published to Slack as a JSON payload. Let's review posting a sensor event to Slack.

8. For example, let's consider posting a message when a cat door opens. The first step is preparing the JSON payload for the message. According to the Slack API documentation (`https://api.slack.com/custom-integrations`), the message payload needs to be in the following format:

```
payload = {"text": "The cat door was just opened!"}
```

9. In order to publish this event, we will make use of the `post()` method from the `requests` module. The data payload needs to be encoded in JSON format while posting it:

```
response = requests.post(URL, json.dumps(payload))
```

10. Putting it all together, we have this:

```
#!/usr/bin/python3

import requests
import json

# generate your own URL
```

```
URL = 'https://hooks.slack.com/services/'

if __name__ == "__main__":
    payload = {"text": "The cat door was just opened!"}
    try:
        # encode data payload and post it
        response = requests.post(URL, json.dumps(payload))
        print(response.text)
    except requests.exceptions.ConnectionError as error:
        print("The error is %s" % error)
```

11. On posting the message, the request returns `ok` as a response. This indicates that the post was successful.

12. Generate your own URL and execute the preceding example (available for download along with this chapter as `slack_post.py`). You will receive a direct message on Slack:

Direct message on Slack

Now, try interfacing a sensor to the Raspberry Pi Zero (discussed in previous chapters) and post the sensor events to Slack.

It is also possible to post sensor events to Twitter and have your Raspberry Pi Zero check for new e-mails and so on. Check this book's website for more examples.

# Flask web framework

In our final section, we will discuss web frameworks in Python. We will discuss the Flask framework (`http://flask.pocoo.org/`). Python-based frameworks enable interfacing sensors to a network using the Raspberry Pi Zero. This enables controlling appliances and reading data from sensors from anywhere within a network. Let's get started!

# Installing Flask

The first step is installing the Flask framework. It can be done as follows:

```
sudo pip3 install flask
```

# Building our first example

The Flask framework documentation explains building the first example. Modify the example from the documentation as follows:

```python
#!/usr/bin/python3

from flask import Flask
app = Flask(__name__)

@app.route("/")
def hello():
    return "Hello World!"

if __name__ == "__main__":
    app.run('0.0.0.0')
```

Launch this example (available for download along with this chapter as `flask_example.py`) and it should launch a server on the Raspberry Pi Zero visible to the network. On another computer, launch a browser and enter the IP address of the Raspberry Pi Zero along with port number, `5000`, as a suffix (as shown in the following snapshot). It should take you to the index page of the server that displays the message **Hello World!**:

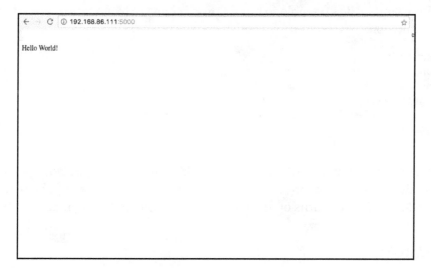

The Flask framework-based web server on the Raspberry Pi Zero

You can find the IP address of your Raspberry Pi Zero using the `ifconfig` command on the command-line terminal.

# Controlling appliances using the Flask framework

Let's try turning on/off appliances at home using the Flask framework. In previous chapters, we made use of *PowerSwitch Tail II* to control a table lamp using the Raspberry Pi Zero. Let's try to control the same using the Flask framework. Connect PowerSwitch Tail, as shown in the following figure:

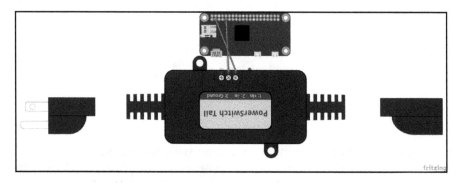

Controlling a table lamp using the Flask framework

According to the Flask framework documentation, it is possible to route a URL to a specific function. For example, it is possible to bind /lamp/<control> using route() to the control() function:

```
@app.route("/lamp/<control>")
def control(control):
  if control == "on":
    lights.on()
  elif control == "off":
    lights.off()
  return "Table lamp is now %s" % control
```

In the preceding code snippet, <control> is a variable that can be passed on as an argument to the binding function. This enables us to turn the lamp on/off. For example, <IP address>:5000/lamp/on turns on the lamp, and vice versa. Putting it all together, we have this:

```
#!/usr/bin/python3

from flask import Flask
from gpiozero import OutputDevice

app = Flask(__name__)
lights = OutputDevice(2)
```

```
@app.route("/lamp/<control>")
def control(control):
    if control == "on":
        lights.on()
    elif control == "off":
        lights.off()
    return "Table lamp is now %s" % control

if __name__ == "__main__":
    app.run('0.0.0.0')
```

The preceding example is available for download along with this chapter as
`appliance_control.py`. Launch the Flask-based web server and open a web server on
another computer. In order to turn on the lamp, enter `<IP Address of the Raspberry
Pi Zero>:5000/lamp/on` as URL:

This should turn on the lamp:

Thus, we have built a simple framework that enables controlling appliances within the
network. It is possible to include buttons to an HTML page and route them to a specific
URL to perform a specific function. There are several other frameworks in Python that
enable developing web applications. We have merely introduced you to different
applications that are possible with Python. We recommend that you check out this book's
website for more examples, such as controlling Halloween decorations and other holiday
decorations using the Flask framework.

# Summary

In this chapter, we discussed the `try/except` keywords in Python. We also discussed
developing applications that retrieves information from the Internet, as well as publishing
sensor events to the Internet. We also discussed the Flask web framework for Python and
demonstrated the control of appliances within a network. In the next chapter, we will
discuss some advanced topics in Python.

# 8

# Awesome Things You Could Develop Using Python

In this chapter, we will discuss some advanced topics in Python. We will also discuss certain unique topics (such as image processing) that let you get started with application development in Python.

## Image processing using a Raspberry Pi Zero

The Raspberry Pi Zero is an inexpensive piece of hardware that is powered by a 1 GHz processor. While it is not powerful to run certain advanced image processing operations, it can help you learn the basics on a $25 budget (the cost of Raspberry Pi Zero and a camera).

 We recommend using a 16 GB card (or higher) with your Raspberry Pi Zero in order to install the image processing tool set discussed in this section.

For example, you could use a Raspberry Pi Zero to track a bird in your backyard. In this chapter, we are going to discuss different ways to get started with image processing on the Raspberry Pi Zero.

In order to test some examples using the camera in this section, a Raspberry Pi Zero v1.3 or later is required. Check the back of your Raspberry Pi Zero to verify the board version:

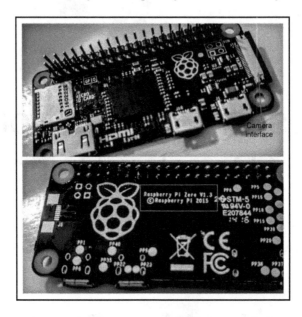

Identifying your Raspberry Pi Zero's version

# OpenCV

**OpenCV** is an open source toolbox that consists of different software tools developed for image processing. OpenCV is a cross-platform toolbox that has been developed with support for different operating systems. Because OpenCV is available under an open source license, researchers across the world have contributed to its growth by developing tools and techniques. This has made developing applications with relative ease. Some applications of OpenCV include face recognition and license plate recognition.

Due to its limited processing power, it can take several hours to complete the installation of the framework. It took us approximately 10 hours at our end.

We followed the instructions to install OpenCV on the Raspberry Pi Zero from `http://www.pyimagesearch.com/2015/10/26/how-to-install-opencv-3-on-raspbian-jessie/`.We specifically followed the instructions to install OpenCV with Python 3.x bindings and verified the installation process. It took us approximately 10 hours to finish installing OpenCV on the Raspberry Pi Zero. We are not repeating the instructions in the interest of not reinventing the wheel.

# The verification of the installation

Let's make sure that the OpenCV installation and its Python bindings work. Launch the command-line terminal and make sure that you have launched the cv virtual environment by executing the `workon cv` command (you can verify that you are in the cv virtual environment):

Verify that you are in the cv virtual environment

Now, let's make sure that our installation works correctly. Launch the Python interpreter from the command line and try to import the cv2 module:

```
>>> import cv2
>>> cv2.__version__
'3.0.0'
```

This proves that OpenCV is installed on the Raspberry Pi Zero. Let's write a *hello world* example involving OpenCV. In this example, we are going to open an image (this can be any color image on your Raspberry Pi Zero's desktop) and display it after converting it to grayscale. We will be using the following documentation to write our first example: `http://docs.opencv.org/3.0-beta/doc/py_tutorials/py_gui/py_image_display/py_image_display.html`.

According to the documentation, we need to make use of the `imread()` function to read the contents of the image file. We also need to specify the format in which we would like to read the image. In this case, we are going to read the image in grayscale format. This is specified by `cv2.IMREAD_GRAYSCALE` that is passed as the second argument to the function:

```
import cv2

img = cv2.imread('/home/pi/screenshot.jpg',cv2.IMREAD_GRAYSCALE)
```

Now that the image is loaded in grayscale format and saved to the `img` variable, we need to display it in a new window. This is enabled by the `imshow()` function. According to the documentation, we can display an image by specifying the window name as the first argument and the image as the second argument:

```
cv2.imshow('image',img)
```

In this case, we are going to open a window named `image` and display the contents of `img` that we loaded in the previous step. We will display the image until a keystroke is received. This is achieved using the `cv2.waitKey()` function. According to the documentation, the `waitkey()` function listens for keyboard events:

```
cv2.waitKey(0)
```

The `0` argument indicates that we are going to wait indefinitely for a keystroke. According to the documentation, when the duration, in milliseconds, is passed as an argument, the `waitkey()` function listens to keystrokes for the specified duration. When any key is pressed, the window is closed by the `destroyAllWindows()` function:

```
cv2.destroyAllWindows()
```

Putting it all together, we have this:

```
import cv2

img = cv2.imread('/home/pi/screenshot.jpg',cv2.IMREAD_GRAYSCALE)
cv2.imshow('image',img)
cv2.waitKey(0)
cv2.destroyAllWindows()
```

The preceding code sample is available for download along with this chapter as
`opencv_test.py`. Once you are done installing OpenCV libraries, try loading an image as
shown in this example. It should load an image in grayscale, as shown in the following
figure:

The Raspberry Pi desktop loaded in grayscale

This window would close at the press of any key.

## A challenge to the reader

In the preceding example, the window closes at the press of any key. Take a look at the
documentation and determine if it is possible to close all windows at the press of a mouse
button.

# Installing the camera to the Raspberry Zero

A camera connector and a camera is required for testing our next example. One source to buy the camera and the adapter is provided here:

| Name | Source |
|------|--------|
| Raspberry Pi Zero camera adapter | `https://thepihut.com/products/raspberry-pi-zero-camera-adapter` |
| Raspberry Pi camera | `https://thepihut.com/products/raspberry-pi-camera-module` |

Perform the following steps to install a camera to the Raspberry Pi Zero:

1. The first step is interfacing the camera to the Raspberry Pi Zero. The camera adapter can be installed as shown in the following figure. Lift the connector tab and slide the camera adapter and press the connector gently:

2. We need to enable the camera interface on the Raspberry Pi Zero. On your desktop, go to **Preferences** and launch **Raspberry Pi Configuration**. Under the **Interfaces** tab of the Raspberry Pi configuration, enable the camera, and save the configuration:

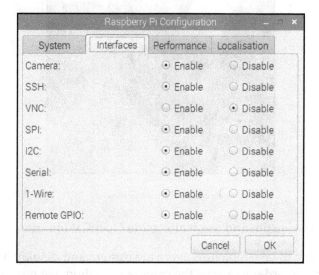

Enable the camera interface

3. Let's test the camera by taking a picture by running the following command from the command-line terminal:

```
raspistill -o /home/pi/Desktop/test.jpg
```

4. It should take a picture and save it to your Raspberry Pi's desktop. Verify that the camera is functioning correctly. If you are not able to get the camera working, we recommend the troubleshooting guide published by the Raspberry Pi Foundation:
https://www.raspberrypi.org/documentation/raspbian/applications/camera.md.

The camera cable is a bit unwieldy, and it can make things difficult while trying to take a picture. We recommend using a camera mount. We found this one to be useful (shown in the following image) at `http://a.co/hQolR7O`:

Use a mount for your Raspberry Pi's camera

Let's take the camera for a spin and use it alongside OpenCV libraries:

1. We are going to take a picture using the camera and display it using the OpenCV framework. In order to access the camera in Python, we need the `picamera` package. This can be installed as follows:

```
pip3 install picamera
```

2. Let's make sure that the package works as intended with a simple program. The documentation for the `picamera` package is available at
`https://picamera.readthedocs.io/en/release-1.12/api_camera.html`.

3. The first step is initializing the `PiCamera` class. This is followed by flipping the image across the vertical axis. This is only required because the camera is mounted upside down on the mount. This may not be necessary with other mounts:

```
with PiCamera() as camera:
    camera.vflip = True
```

4. Before taking a picture, we can preview the picture that is going to be captured using the `start_preview()` method:

```
camera.start_preview()
```

5. Let's preview for `10` seconds before we take a picture. We can take a picture using the `capture()` method:

```
sleep(10)
camera.capture("/home/pi/Desktop/desktop_shot.jpg")
camera.stop_preview()
```

6. The `capture()` method requires the file location as an argument (as shown in the preceding snippet). Once we are done, we can close the camera preview using `stop_preview()`.

7. Putting it altogether, we have this:

```
from picamera import PiCamera
from time import sleep

if __name__ == "__main__":
    with PiCamera() as camera:
        camera.vflip = True
        camera.start_preview()
        sleep(10)
        camera.capture("/home/pi/Desktop/desktop_shot.jpg")
        camera.stop_preview()
```

The preceding code sample is available for download along with this chapter as `picamera_test.py`. A snapshot taken using the camera is shown in the following figure:

Image captured using the Raspberry Pi camera module

8. Let's combine this example with the previous one—convert this image to grayscale and display it until a key is pressed. Ensure that you are still within the `cv` virtual environment workspace.

9. Let's convert the captured image to grayscale as follows:

```
img = cv2.imread("/home/pi/Desktop/desktop_shot.jpg",
cv2.IMREAD_GRAYSCALE)
```

The following is the image converted upon capture:

Image converted to grayscale upon capture

10. Now we can display the grayscale image as follows:

```
cv2.imshow("image", img)
cv2.waitKey(0)
cv2.destroyAllWindows()
```

The modified example is available for download as `picamera_opencvtest.py`.

So far, we have demonstrated developing image processing applications in Python. In Chapter 10, *Home Automation Using the Raspberry Pi Zero*, we have demonstrated another example using OpenCV. This should get you kick-started with learning OpenCV in Python. We also recommend checking out examples available with the OpenCV Python binding documentation (link provided in the introduction part of this section).

# Speech recognition

In this section, we will discuss developing a speech recognition example in Python involving speech recognition. We will make use of the requests module (discussed in the previous chapter) to transcribe audio using wit.ai (https://wit.ai/).

 There are several speech recognition tools, including Google's Speech API, IBM Watson, Microsoft Bing's speech recognition API. We are demonstrating wit.ai as an example.

Speech recognition can be useful in applications where we would like to enable the Raspberry Pi Zero responses to voice commands. For example, in Chapter 10, *Home Automation Using the Raspberry Pi Zero*, we will be working on a home automation project. We could make use of speech recognition to respond to voice commands.

Let's review building the speech recognition application in Python using wit.ai (its documentation is available here at https://github.com/wit-ai/pywit). In order to perform speech recognition and recognize voice commands, we will need a microphone. However, we will demonstrate using a readily available audio sample. We will make use of audio samples made available by a research publication (available at http://ecs.utdallas.edu/loizou/speech/noizeus/clean.zip).

 The wit.ai API license states that the tool is free to use, but the audio uploaded to their servers are used to tune their speech transcription tool.

We will now attempt transcribing the `sp02.wav` audio sample performing the following steps:

1. The first step is signing up for an account with `wit.ai`. Make a note of the API as shown in the following screenshot:

2. The first step is installing the requests library. It could be installed as follows:

   ```
   pip3 install requests
   ```

3. According to the `wit.ai` documentation, we need to add custom headers to our request that includes the API key (replace `$TOKEN` with the token from your account). We also need to specify the file format in the header. In this case, it is a `.wav` file, and the sampling frequency is 8000 Hz:

   ```python
   import requests

   if __name__ == "__main__":
       url = 'https://api.wit.ai/speech?v=20161002'
       headers = {"Authorization": "Bearer $TOKEN",
                  "Content-Type": "audio/wav"}
   ```

4. In order to transcribe the audio sample, we need to attach the audio sample in the request body:

   ```python
   files = open('sp02.wav', 'rb')
   response = requests.post(url, headers=headers, data=files)
   print(response.status_code)
   print(response.text)
   ```

5.  Putting it all together, gives us this:

```python
#!/usr/bin/python3

import requests

if __name__ == "__main__":
    url = 'https://api.wit.ai/speech?v=20161002'
    headers = {"Authorization": "Bearer $TOKEN",
               "Content-Type": "audio/wav"}
    files = open('sp02.wav', 'rb')
    response = requests.post(url, headers=headers, data=files)
    print(response.status_code)
    print(response.text)
```

The preceding code sample is available for download along with this chapter as
wit_ai.py. Try executing the preceding code sample, and it should transcribe the audio
sample: sp02.wav. We have the following code:

```
200
{
  "msg_id" : "fae9cc3a-f7ed-4831-87ba-6a08e95f515b",
  "_text" : "he knew the the great young actress",
  "outcomes" : [ {
    "_text" : "he knew the the great young actress",
    "confidence" : 0.678,
    "intent" : "DataQuery",
    "entities" : {
      "value" : [ {
        "confidence" : 0.7145905790744499,
        "type" : "value",
        "value" : "he",
        "suggested" : true
      }, {
        "confidence" : 0.5699616515542044,
        "type" : "value",
        "value" : "the",
        "suggested" : true
      }, {
        "confidence" : 0.5981701138805214,
        "type" : "value",
        "value" : "great",
        "suggested" : true
      }, {
        "confidence" : 0.8999612482250062,
        "type" : "value",
        "value" : "actress",
        "suggested" : true
```

```
      } ]
    }
  } ],
  "WARNING" : "DEPRECATED"
}
```

The audio sample contains the following recording: *He knew the skill of the great young actress*. According to the `wit.ai` API, the transcription is *He knew the the great young actress*. The word error rate is 22% (`https://en.wikipedia.org/wiki/Word_error_rate`).

 We will be making use of the speech transcription API to issue voice commands in our home automation project.

# Automating routing tasks

In this section, we are going to discuss automating routing tasks in Python. We took two examples such that they demonstrate the ability of a Raspberry Pi Zero acting as a personal assistant. The first example involves improving your commute, whereas the second example serves as an aid to improve your vocabulary. Let's get started.

# Improving daily commute

Many cities and public transit systems have started sharing data with the public in the interest of being transparent and improving their operational efficiency. Transit systems have started sharing advisories and transit information to the public through an API. This enables anyone to develop mobile applications that provide information to commuters. At times, it helps with easing congestion within the public transit system.

This example was inspired by a friend who tracks bicycle availability in San Francisco's bike share stations. In the San Francisco Bay Area, there is a bicycle sharing program that enables commuters to rent a bike from a transit center to their work. In a crowded city like San Francisco, bike availability at a given station fluctuates depending on the time of day.

This friend wanted to plan his day based on bike availability at the nearest bike share station. If there are very few bikes left at the station, this friend preferred leaving early to rent a bike. He was looking for a simple hack that would push a notification to his phone when the number of bikes is below a certain threshold. San Francisco's bike share program makes this data available at
`http://feeds.bayareabikeshare.com/stations/stations.json.`

Let's review building a simple example that would enable sending a push notification to a mobile device. In order to send a mobile push notification, we will be making use of **If This Then That (IFTTT)**—a service that enables connecting your project to third-party services.

In this example, we will parse the data available in JSON format, check the number of available bikes at a specific station, and if it is lower than the specified threshold, it triggers a notification on your mobile device.

Let's get started:

1. The first step is retrieving the bike availability from the bike share service. This data is available in JSON format at
   `http://feeds.bayareabikeshare.com/stations/stations.json`. The data includes bike availability throughout the network.
2. The bike availability at each station is provided with parameters, such as station ID, station name, address, number of bikes available, and so on.
3. In this example, we will retrieve the bike availability for the `Townsend at 7th` station in San Francisco. The station ID is `65` (open the earlier-mentioned link in a browser to find `id`). Let's write some Python code to retrieve the bike availability data and parse this information:

   ```
   import requests

   BIKE_URL = http://feeds.bayareabikeshare.com/stations
   /stations.json

   # fetch the bike share information
   response = requests.get(BIKE_URL)
   parsed_data = response.json()
   ```

The first step is fetching the data using a `GET` request (via the `requests` module). The `requests` module provides an inbuilt JSON decoder. The JSON data can be parsed by calling the `json()` function.

4. Now, we can iterate through the dictionary of stations and find the bike availability at `Townsend at 7th`, by performing the following steps:

   1. In the retrieved data, each station's data is furnished with an ID. The station ID in question is `65` (open the data feed URL provided earlier in a browser to understand the data format; a snippet of the data is shown in the following screenshot):

```
{"id":65,"stationName":"Townsend at 7th","availableDocks":7,"totalDocks"
```

A snippet of the bike share data feed fetched using a browser

   2. We need to iterate through the values and determine if the station `id` matches that of `Townsend at 7th`:

```python
station_list = parsed_data['stationBeanList']
for station in station_list:
  if station['id'] == 65 and
    station['availableBikes'] < 2:
   print("The available bikes is %d" % station
   ['availableBikes'])
```

   3. If there are less than `2` bikes available at the station, we push a mobile notification to our mobile device.

5. In order to receive mobile notifications, you need to install *IF by IFTTT* app (available for Apple and Android devices).

6. We also need to set up a recipe on IFTTT to trigger mobile notifications. Sign up for an account at `https://ifttt.com/`.

IFTTT is a service that enables creating recipes that connecting devices to different applications and automating tasks. For example, it is possible to log events tracked by the Raspberry Pi Zero to a spreadsheet on your Google Drive.

All recipes on IFTTT follow a common template—*if this then that*, that is, if a particular event has occurred, then a specific action is triggered. For this example, we need to create an applet that triggers a mobile notification on receiving a web request.

7. You can start creating an applet using the drop-down menu under your account, as shown in the following screenshot:

Start creating a recipe on IFTTT

8. It should take you to a recipe setup page (shown as follows). Click on **this** and set up an incoming web request:

Click on this

9. Select the **Maker Webhooks** channel as the incoming trigger:

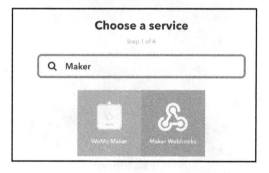

Select the Maker Webhooks channel

10. Select **Receive a web request**. A web request from the Raspberry Pi would act as a trigger to send a mobile notification:

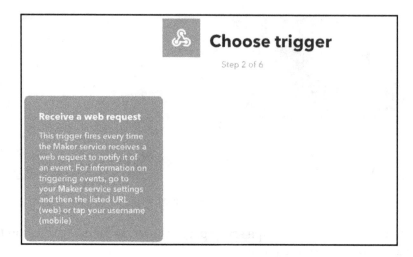

Select Receive a web request

11. Create a trigger named `mobile_notify`:

Create a new trigger named mobile_notify

12. It is time to create an action for the incoming trigger. Click on **that**.

Click on that

13. Select **Notifications**:

Select Notifications

14. Now, let's format the notification that we would like to receive on our devices:

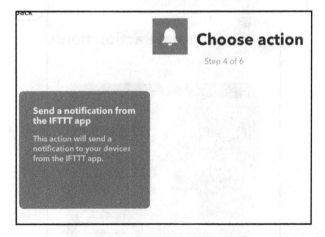

Setup notification for your device

15. In the mobile notification, we need to receive the number of bikes available at the bike share station. Click on the **+ Ingredient** button and select `Value1`.

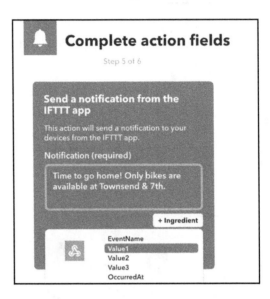

Format the message to suit your needs. For example, when a notification is triggered by the Raspberry Pi, it would be great to receive a message in the following format: `Time to go home! Only 2 bikes are available at Townsend & 7th!`

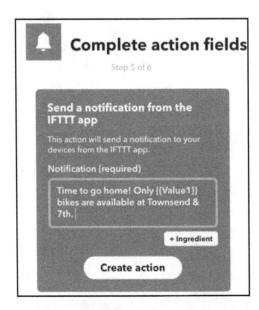

16. Once you are satisfied with the message format, select **Create action** and your recipe should be ready!

Create a recipe

17. In order to trigger a notification on our mobile device, we need a URL to make the POST request and a trigger key. This is available under **Services** | **Maker Webhooks** | **Settings** in your IFTTT account.

The trigger can be located here:

Open the URL listed in the preceding screenshot in a new browser window. It provides the URL for the POST request as well as an explanation on (shown in the following screenshot) how to make a web request:

## Your key is:
◀ Back to service

### To trigger an Event

Make a POST or GET web request to:

`https://maker.ifttt.com/trigger/` `{event}` `/with/key/`

With an optional JSON body of:

`{ "value1" : "_____", "value2" : "_____", "value3" : "_____" }`

The data is completely optional, and you can also pass value1, value2, and value3 as query parameters or form variables. This content will be passed on to the Action in your Recipe.

You can also try it with curl from a command line.

`curl -X POST https://maker.ifttt.com/trigger/{event}/with/key/`

**Test It**

Making a POST request using the earlier-mentioned URL (key concealed for privacy)

18. While making a request (as explained in the IFTTT documentation), if we include the number of bikes in the JSON body of request (using Value1), it can be shown on the mobile notification.

19. Let's revisit the Python example to make a web request when the number of bikes is below a certain threshold. Save the IFTTT URL and your IFTTT access key (retrieved from your IFTTT account) to your code as follows:

```
IFTTT_URL = "https://maker.ifttt.com/trigger/mobile_notify/
with/key/$KEY"
```

20. When the number of bikes is below a certain threshold, we need to make a POST request with the bike information encoded in the JSON body:

```
for station in station_list:
    if station['id'] == 65 and
        station['availableBikes'] < 3:
        print("The available bikes is %d" %
```

```
        station['availableBikes'])
      payload = {"value1": station['availableBikes']}
      response = requests.post(IFTTT_URL, json=payload)
      if response.status_code == 200:
        print("Notification successfully triggered")
```

21. In the preceding code snippet, if there are less than three bikes, a POST request is
    made using the requests module. The number of available bikes is encoded
    with the key value1:

    ```
    payload = {"value1": station['availableBikes']}
    ```

22. Putting it all together, we have this:

    ```
    #!/usr/bin/python3

    import requests
    import datetime

    BIKE_URL = "http://feeds.bayareabikeshare.com/stations/
    stations.json"
    # find your key from ifttt
    IFTTT_URL = "https://maker.ifttt.com/trigger/mobile_notify/
    with/key/$KEY"

    if __name__ == "__main__":
      # fetch the bike share information
      response = requests.get(BIKE_URL)
      parsed_data = response.json()
      station_list = parsed_data['stationBeanList']
      for station in station_list:
        if station['id'] == 65 and
            station['availableBikes'] < 10:
          print("The available bikes is %d" % station
          ['availableBikes'])
      payload = {"value1": station['availableBikes']}
          response = requests.post(IFTTT_URL, json=payload)
          if response.status_code == 200:
            print("Notification successfully triggered")
    ```

The preceding code sample is available for download along with this chapter as `bike_share.py`. Try executing it after setting up a recipe on IFTTT. If necessary, adjust the threshold for the number of available bikes. You should receive a mobile notification on your device:

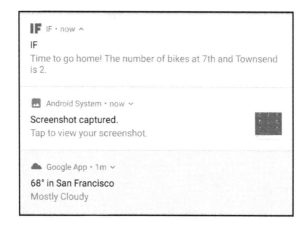

Notification on your mobile device

# A challenge to the reader

In this example, the bike information is fetched and parsed and if necessary, a notification is triggered. How would you go about modifying this code example to make sure that it is executed between a given time of the day? (hint: make use of `datetime` module).

How would you go about building a desktop display that serves as a visual aid?

# Project challenge

Try to find out if the transit systems in your area provide such data to its users. How would you make use of the data to help commuters save time? For example, how would you provide transit system advisories to your friends/colleagues using such data?

 On completion of the book, we will post a similar example using the data from San Francisco **Bay Area Rapid Transit** (**BART**).

# Improving your vocabulary

It is possible to improve your vocabulary using Python! Imagine setting up a large display that is installed somewhere prominently and updated on a daily basis. We will be making use of the wordnik API (sign up for an API key at https://www.wordnik.com/signup):

1. The first step is to install the wordnik API client for python3:

```
git clone https://github.com/wordnik/wordnik-python3.git
cd wordnik-python3/
sudo python3 setup.py install
```

There are restrictions on the wordnik API usage. Refer to the API documentation for more details.

2. Let's review writing our first example using the wordnik Python client. In order to fetch the word of the day, we need to initialize the WordsApi class. According to the API documentation, this could be done as follows:

```
# sign up for an API key
API_KEY = 'API_KEY'
apiUrl = 'http://api.wordnik.com/v4'
client = swagger.ApiClient(API_KEY, apiUrl)
wordsApi = WordsApi.WordsApi(client)
```

3. Now that the WordsApi class is initialized, let's go ahead and fetch the word of the day:

```
example = wordsApi.getWordOfTheDay()
```

4. This returns a WordOfTheDay object. According to the wordnik Python client documentation, this object consists of different parameters including the word, its synonym, source, usage, and so on. The word of the day and its synonym could be printed as follows:

```
print("The word of the day is %s" % example.word)
print("The definition is %s" %example.definitions[0].text)
```

5. Putting it all together, we have this:

```
#!/usr/bin/python3

from wordnik import *

# sign up for an API key
API_KEY = 'API_KEY'
apiUrl = 'http://api.wordnik.com/v4'

if __name__ == "__main__":
    client = swagger.ApiClient(API_KEY, apiUrl)
    wordsApi = WordsApi.WordsApi(client)
    example = wordsApi.getWordOfTheDay()
    print("The word of the day is %s" % example.word)
    print("The definition is %s" %example.definitions[0].text)
```

The preceding code snippet is available for download along with this chapter as wordOfTheDay.py. Sign up for an API key, and you should be able to retrieve the word of the day:

```
The word of the day is transpare
The definition is To be, or cause to be, transparent; to appear,
or cause to appear, or be seen, through something.
```

# A challenge to the reader

How would you daemonize this application such that the word of the day is updated every day? (hint: cronjob or datetime).

# Project challenge

It is possible to build a word game using the wordnik API. Think of a word game that is entertaining as well as helps improve your vocabulary. How would you go about building something that prompts questions to the player and accepting answer inputs?

Try displaying the word of the day on a display. How would you implement this?

# Logging

This is a topic that is going to be useful for the next two chapters. Logging (`https://docs.python.org/3/library/logging.html`) helps with troubleshooting a problem. It helps with determining the root cause of a problem by tracing back through the sequence of events logged by the application. While we will be making extensive use of logging in the next two chapters, let's review logging using a simple application. In order to review logging, let's review it by making a `POST` request:

1. The first step in logging is setting the log file location and the log level:

```
logging.basicConfig(format='%(asctime)s : %(levelname)s :
%(message)s', filename='log_file.log', level=logging.INFO)
```

While initializing the `logging` class, we need to specify the format for logging information, errors, and so on to the file. In this case, the format is as follows:

```
format='%(asctime)s : %(levelname)s : %(message)s'
```

The log messages are in the following format:

```
2016-10-25 20:28:07,940 : INFO : Starting new HTTPS
connection (1):
maker.ifttt.com
```

The log messages are saved to a file named `log_file.log`.

The logging level determines the level of logging needed for our application. The different log levels include `DEBUG`, `INFO`, `WARN`, and `ERROR`.

In this example, we have set the logging level to `INFO`. So, any log message belonging to `INFO`, `WARNING`, or `ERROR` levels are saved to the file.

If the logging level is set to `ERROR`, only those log messages are saved to the file.

2. Let's log a message based on the outcome of the `POST` request:

```
response = requests.post(IFTTT_URL, json=payload)
if response.status_code == 200:
  logging.info("Notification successfully triggered")
else:
  logging.error("POST request failed")
```

3. Putting it all together, we have this:

```
#!/usr/bin/python3

import requests
import logging

# find your key from ifttt
IFTTT_URL = "https://maker.ifttt.com/trigger/rf_trigger/
with/key/$key"

if __name__ == "__main__":
  # fetch the bike share information
  logging.basicConfig(format='%(asctime)s : %(levelname)s
  : %(message)s', filename='log_file.log', level=logging.INFO)
  payload = {"value1": "Sample_1", "value2": "Sample_2"}
  response = requests.post(IFTTT_URL, json=payload)
  if response.status_code == 200:
    logging.info("Notification successfully triggered")
  else:
    logging.error("POST request failed")
```

The preceding code sample (`logging_example.py`) is available for download along with this chapter. This is a very soft introduction to the concept of logging in Python. We are going to make use of logging to troubleshoot any errors in our project.

In the final chapter, we will discuss best practices in logging.

# Threading in Python

In this section, we are going to discuss the concept of threading in Python. We will be making use of threading in the next chapter. Threads enable running multiple processes at the same time. For example, we can run motors while listening to incoming events from sensors. Let's demonstrate this with an example.

We are going to emulate a situation where we would like to process events from sensors of the same type. In this example, we are just going to print something to the screen. We need to define a function that listens to events from each sensor:

```
def sensor_processing(string):
  for num in range(5):
    time.sleep(5)
    print("%s: Iteration: %d" %(string, num))
```

We can make use of the preceding function to listen for sensor events from three different sensors at the same time using the `threading` module in Python:

```
thread_1 = threading.Thread(target=sensor_processing, args=("Sensor 1",))
thread_1.start()

thread_2 = threading.Thread(target=sensor_processing, args=("Sensor 2",))
thread_2.start()

thread_3 = threading.Thread(target=sensor_processing, args=("Sensor 3",))
thread_3.start()
```

Putting it all together, we have this:

```
import threading
import time

def sensor_processing(string):
    for num in range(5):
        time.sleep(5)
        print("%s: Iteration: %d" % (string, num))

if __name__ == '__main__':
    thread_1 = threading.Thread(target=sensor_processing, args=("Sensor 1",))
    thread_1.start()

    thread_2 = threading.Thread(target=sensor_processing, args=("Sensor 2",))
    thread_2.start()

    thread_3 = threading.Thread(target=sensor_processing, args=("Sensor 3",))
    thread_3.start()
```

The preceding code sample (available for download as `threading_example.py`) starts three threads that listens to events from three sensors at the same time. The output looks something like this:

```
Thread 1: Iteration: 0
Thread 2: Iteration: 0
Thread 3: Iteration: 0
Thread 2: Iteration: 1
Thread 1: Iteration: 1
Thread 3: Iteration: 1
Thread 2: Iteration: 2
Thread 1: Iteration: 2
Thread 3: Iteration: 2
Thread 1: Iteration: 3
Thread 2: Iteration: 3
Thread 3: Iteration: 3
```

```
Thread 1: Iteration: 4
Thread 2: Iteration: 4
Thread 3: Iteration: 4
```

In the next chapter, we are going to make use of threading to control the motors of a robot-based on sensor inputs.

# PEP8 style guide for Python

**PEP8** is a style guide for Python that helps programmers write readable code. It is important to follow certain conventions to make our code readable. Some examples of coding conventions include the following:

- Inline comments should start with a # and be followed by a single space.
- Variables should have the following convention: `first_var`.
- Avoiding trailing whitespaces on each line. For example, `if name == "test":` should not be followed by whitespaces.

You can read the entire PEP8 standards at
`https://www.python.org/dev/peps/pep-0008/#block-comments`.

# Verifying PEP8 guidelines

There are tools to verify PEP8 standards of your code. After writing a code sample, ensure that your code adheres to PEP8 standards. This can be done using the `pep8` package. It can be installed as follows:

```
pip3 install pep8
```

Let's check whether one of our code samples has been written according to the PEP8 convention. This can be done as follows:

```
pep8 opencv_test.py
```

The check indicated the following errors:

```
opencv_test.py:5:50: E231 missing whitespace after ','
opencv_test.py:6:19: E231 missing whitespace after ','
```

As the output indicates, the following lines are missing a whitespace after a comma on lines 5 and 6:

```
5    img = cv2.imread('/home/pi/Desktop/test_shot.jpg',cv2.IMREAD_GRAYSCALE)
6    cv2.imshow('image',img)
```

Missing trailing whitespace after the comma

Let's fix the problem, and our code should adhere to PEP8 conventions. Recheck the file and the errors would have disappeared. In order to make your code readable, always run a PEP8 check before checking in your code to a public repository.

# Summary

In this chapter, we discussed advanced topics in Python. We discussed topics including speech recognition, building a commuter information tool, and a Python client to improve your vocabulary. There are advanced tools in Python that are widely used in the fields of data science, AI, and so on. We hope that the topics discussed in this chapter are the first step in learning such tools.

# 9
# Lets Build a Robot!

In this chapter, we built an indoor robot (using the Raspberry Pi Zero as the controller) and documented our experience in a step-by-step guide. We wanted to demonstrate the awesomeness of the combination of Python programming language and the Raspberry Pi Zero's peripherals. We have also included suggestions to build an outdoor robot as well as suggestions for additional accessories for your robot. At the end of this chapter, we have included additional learning resources to build your own robot. Let's get started!

In this chapter, we are going to access the Raspberry Pi Zero via remote login (SSH) and remotely transferred files from the Raspberry Pi Zero. If you are not familiar with the command-line interface, we recommend proceeding to Chapter 11, *Tips and Tricks*, to set up your local desktop environment.

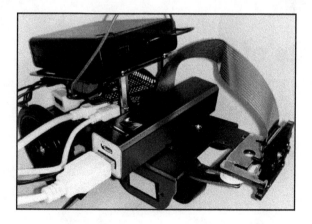

A Raspberry Pi Zero powered robot

Since we will be making use of a camera for our robot, Raspberry Pi Zero v1.3 or higher is needed for this chapter. Your Raspberry Pi Zero's board version is available on the back. Refer to the following picture:

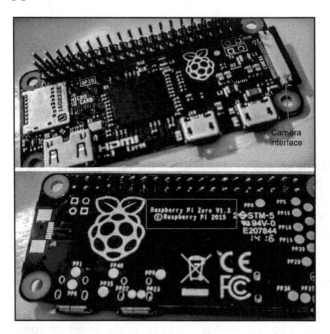

Identifying your Raspberry Pi Zero's version

# Components of the robot

Let's discuss the components of the robot using the labeled picture as an aid (shown in the following figure):

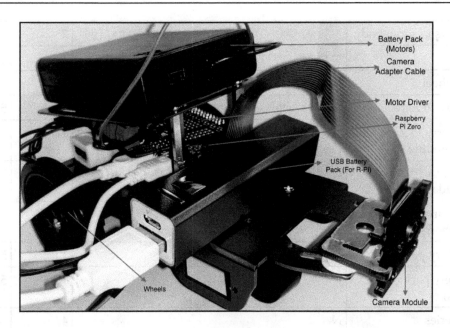

Components of the robot

The following is an explanation for the components of the robot:

- The Raspberry Pi Zero controls the movement of the robot using a motor driver circuit (stacked on top of the Raspberry Pi Zero)
- The motors of the robot are connected to the motor driver circuit
- A USB battery pack is used to power the Raspberry Pi Zero. A separate AA battery pack is used to drive the motors
- The robot is also equipped with a camera module that helps with driving the robot

We have included a suggested list of components where we chose the cheapest source available for the component. You are welcome to substitute with your own components. For example, you can use a webcam instead of using the Raspberry Pi camera module:

| Component | Source | Quantity | Price (in USD) |
| --- | --- | --- | --- |
| Chassis | https://www.adafruit.com/products/2943 | 1 | 9.95 |
| Chassis top plate | https://www.adafruit.com/products/2944 | 1 | 4.95 |
| A set of M2.5 rows, spacers, and nuts | http://a.co/dpdmb1B | 1 | 11.99 |

| DC motors in servo body | https://www.adafruit.com/products/2941 | 2 | 3.50 |
| Wheel | https://www.adafruit.com/products/2744 | 2 | 2.50 |
| Castor wheel | https://www.adafruit.com/products/2942 | 1 | 1.95 |
| Raspberry Pi Zero | https://www.adafruit.com/products/3400 | 1 | 5.00 |
| A Raspberry Pi Zero camera module | http://a.co/07iFhxC | 1 | 24.99 |
| A Raspberry Pi Zero camera adapter | https://www.adafruit.com/products/3157 | 1 | 5.95 |
| A motor driver circuitry for Raspberry Pi Zero | https://www.adafruit.com/products/2348 | 1 | 22.50 |
| USB battery pack | http://a.co/9vQLx2t | 1 | 5.09 |
| AA battery pack (4 batteries) | http://a.co/hVPxfzD | 1 | 5.18 |
| AA batteries | NA | 4 | N.A. |
| Raspberry Pi camera module mount | https://www.adafruit.com/products/1434 | 1 | 4.95 |

In the interest of saving time, we chose off-the-shelf accessories to build robot. We specifically chose Adafruit for the ease of purchase and shipping. If you are interested in building a robot that needs to suit outdoor conditions, we recommend a chassis similar to http://www.robotshop.com/en/iron-man-3-4wd-all-terrain-chassis-arduino.html.

As makers, we recommend making your own chassis and control circuitry (especially the motor drive). You can make use of software such as Autodesk Fusion (the link is available in the resources section) to design the chassis.

# Setting up remote login

To control the robot remotely, we need to set up remote login access, that is, enable the SSH access. **Secure Shell** (**SSH**), and it is a protocol that enables remote access of a computer. The SSH access is disabled by default on the Raspbian operating system for security reasons. In this section, we will enable the SSH access to the Raspberry Pi Zero and change the Raspberry Pi Zero's default password.

If you are not familiar with the SSH access, we have provided a quick tutorial in `Chapter 11`, *Tips and Tricks*. We would like to keep the focus on building the robot in this chapter.

# Changing the password

Before we enable the SSH access, we need to change the default password of the Raspberry Pi Zero. This is to avoid any potential threat to your computer and your robot! We have advocated changing default passwords on multiple occasions in this chapter. Default passwords have wreaked havoc across the Internet.

 Recommended reading *Mirai botnet attack*:
`http://fortune.com/2016/10/23/internet-attack-perpetrator/.`

On your desktop, go to **Menu** | **Preferences** and launch **Raspberry Pi Configuration**. Under the **System** tab, there is an option to change the password under the **System** tab (shown in the following screenshot):

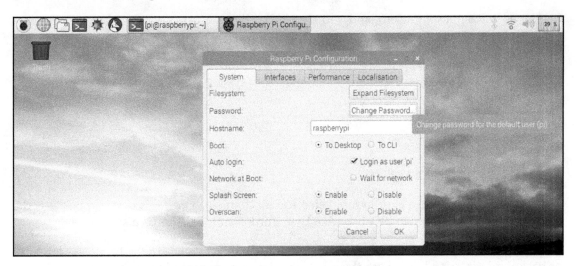

Change your Raspberry Pi Zero's default password

# Enabling SSH access

Under the **Interfaces** tab of the Raspberry Pi configuration, select **Enable** for **SSH** (as shown in the following screenshot):

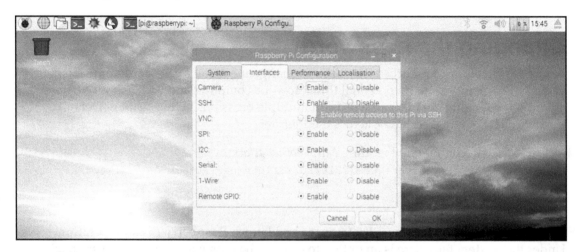

Enable SSH under the Interfaces tab

Reboot your Raspberry Pi Zero, and you should be able to access your Raspberry Pi Zero via SSH.

 Refer to Chapter 11, *Tips and Tricks*, for the SSH access to your Raspberry Pi Zero from Windows, *nix operating systems (beyond the scope of this chapter).

# Chassis setup

The robot is going to have a differential steering mechanism. Thus, it is going to be steered by two motors. It is going to be supported by a third castor that acts as a support.

In a differential steering mechanism arrangement, the robot moves in the forward direction or backward direction when both the wheels of the robot are rotating in the same direction. The robot can turn left or right by rotating one wheel faster than the other wheel. For example, in order to rotate left, the right motor needs to rotate faster than the left and vice versa.

In order to reach a better understanding of the differential steering mechanism, we recommend building out the chassis and testing it with the Raspberry Pi Zero (We are going to test our chassis using a simple program in the later part of this chapter).

We have provided additional resources on differential steering at the end of this chapter.

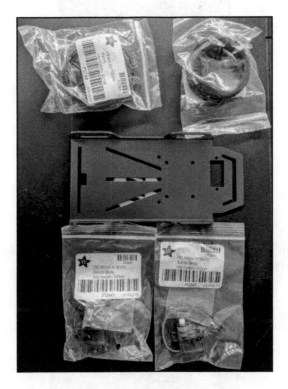

Chassis prep for the robot

1. The chassis comes with the required provisions along with the screws required to mount the motors. Ensure that the motor's wires are facing the same side (Refer to the picture given later). Similarly, the castor wheel can be assembled at the front, as shown in the picture here:

Assemble motors and mount castor wheels

2. The next step is mounting the wheels. The wheels are designed to be press-fitted directly onto the motor shaft.

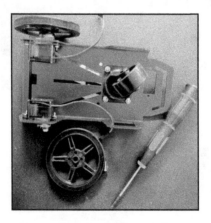

Assembling wheels onto the servo

3. Lock the wheels in place using a screw (comes with the wheels)

Lock the wheel onto the shaft

Thus, we are done setting up the chassis for the robot. Let's move on to the next section.

# Motor driver and motor selection

The motor driver circuit (https://www.adafruit.com/product/2348) can be used to connect four DC motors or two stepper motors. The motor driver is rated to provide 1.2A of current per motor under continuous operation. This sufficiently meets the robot's motor power requirement.

# Preparing the motor driver circuit

The motor driver circuit comes as a kit, and it requires some soldering (shown in the figure here).

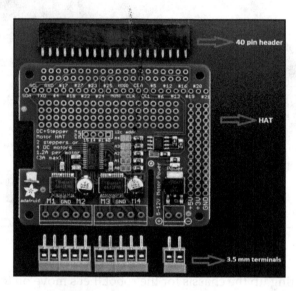

Adafruit DC and Stepper Motor HAT for Raspberry Pi-Mini Kit (picture source: adafruit.com)

1. The first step in the assembly process is to solder the **40 pin header**. Stack the header on top of your Raspberry Pi Zero and as shown in the picture here:

Stack the header on top of the Raspberry Pi Zero

2. Position the motor driver (as shown in the picture here) on top of the header. Hold on to the motor driver board so that the board is not tilted while soldering.

Stack the motor HAT on top of the Raspberry Pi Zero

3. Solder the corner pins of the motor driver first and proceed to solder the other pins.

Note the motor driver board soldered such that the board is parallel to the Raspberry Pi Zero

4. Now, solder the 3.5 mm terminals (see the blue colored ones in the picture) by flipping the board

Solder the 3.5 mm terminals

5. The motor driver board is ready to use!

The motor driver is ready to use

# Raspberry Pi Zero and motor driver assembly

In this section, we are going to test the movements of the robot. This includes testing the motor driver and basic movements of the robot.

# Raspberry Pi Zero and motor driver assembly

In this section, we are going to assemble the Raspberry Pi Zero and the motor driver on to the robot chassis.

1. In order to mount the Raspberry Pi Zero on to the chassis, we need 4 M2.5 screws and nuts (Mounting hole specification available at
   `https://www.raspberrypi.org/documentation/hardware/raspberrypi/mechanical/rpi-zero-v1_2_dimensions.pdf`).
2. The chassis we selected comes with slots that enables mounting the Raspberry Pi Zero directly on to the chassis. Based on your chassis design, you may have to drill clearance holes to mount the Raspberry Pi Zero.

Mounting the Raspberry Pi Zero onto the chassis

 While mounting the Raspberry Pi Zero, we ensured that we are able to plug in the HDMI cable, USB cable, and so on for testing purposes.

3. The chassis we have used is made of anodized aluminum;hence, it is nonconductive. We mounted the Raspberry Pi Zero directly, without any insulation between the chassis and the Raspberry Pi Zero.

Ensure that you don't short circuit any component by accidentally exposing them directly to conductive metal surfaces.

4. Stack the motor driver on top of the Raspberry Pi Zero (as shown in the previous section).
5. The two motors of the robot need to be connected to the Raspberry Pi Zero:
6. The motor driver comes with motor terminals M1 through M4. Let's connect the left and right DC motors to M1 and M2, respectively.

Red and black wires connected from both the motors to the motor driver terminals

7. Each motor comes with two terminals, that is, black wire and a red wire. Connect the black wire to the left-most terminal of the bridge M1 and the red wire to the right-hand side terminal of the bridge M1 (as shown in the picture earlier). Similarly, the right motor is connected to the bridge M2.

Now, that we have connected the motors, we need to test the motor function and verify that the motors are rotating in the same direction. In order to do so, we need to set up the robot's power supply.

# Robot Power supply setup

In this section, we will discuss setting up the power supply for the Raspberry Pi Zero. We will discuss powering the Raspberry Pi Zero and the motors of the robot. Let's discuss the major components of our robot and their power consumption:

- The Raspberry Pi Zero requires a 5V power supply, and it draws about 150 mA of current (Source: `http://raspberrypi.stackexchange.com/a/40393/1470`).
- The two DC motors of the robot consume about 150 mA each.
- The camera module consumes 250 mA of current (Source: `https://www.raspberrypi.org/help/faqs/#cameraPower`).

The total power consumption estimate is about 550 mA (150 + 150*2 + 250).

In order to calculate the battery capacity, we also need to decide the duration of continuous operation before requiring a recharge. We wanted the robot to operate at least for 2 hours before requiring a recharge. The battery capacity can be calculated using the following formula:

$$\text{Battery capacity} = \text{Power consumption} * \text{Battery life time}$$

In our case, this would be:

*550mA * 2 hours = 1100 mAh*

 We also found a battery life calculator from Digi-Key:
`http://www.digikey.com/en/resources/conversion-calculators/conversion-calculator-battery-life`

According to the Digi-Key calculator, we need to account for factors that affect the battery life. Accounting for such factors, the battery capacity would be:

*1100 mAh /0.7 = 1571.42 mAh*

We took this number into account while purchasing a battery for the robot. We decided to purchase this `2200mAh` USB battery pack that operates at 5V (shown in the picture later and the link for purchase has been shared with the bill of materials discussed earlier in this chapter):

2200 mAh 5V USB battery pack

Ensure that the battery pack is fully charged before assembling it on to the robot:

1. Once the battery pack is fully charged, mount it on to the robot using double-sided tape and plug a micro-USB cable, as shown in the picture:

2200 mAh 5V USB battery pack

2. We need to verify that the Raspberry Pi Zero powers up when a battery pack is used.

3. Plug in the HDMI cable (that is connected to a monitor) and using a very short micro-USB cable, try to power up the Raspberry Pi Zero and make sure that everything powers up correctly.

# Setting up the motor power supply

Now that we have set up the power supply for the robot and verified that the Raspberry Pi Zero powers up using the USB battery pack, we will discuss power supply options to drive the motors of the robot. We are discussing this because the type of motor, and its power supply determines the performance of our robot. Let's get started!

Let's revisit the motor driver that we set up in the previous section. The unique feature of this motor driver is that it is equipped with its own voltage regulator and polarity protection. Thus, it enables connecting an external power supply to power the motors (shown in the picture here)

Motor driver power terminals

This motor driver enables driving any motor with a voltage requirement of 5-12V and current rating of 1.2A. There are two options to power the motors of your robot:

- Using the Raspberry Pi Zero's 5V GPIO power supply
- Using an external power supply

## Using the Raspberry Pi Zero's 5V power supply

The motor driver is designed such that it can act as a prototyping platform. There is a bank of 5V and 3.3V power supply pins that is connected to the Raspberry Pi Zero's 5V and 3.3V GPIO pins. These GPIO pins are rated to provide a current of 1.5A (Source: `https://pinout.xyz/pinout/pin2_5v_power`). They are directly connected to the 5V USB input of your Raspberry Pi Zero. (The USB battery pack used in this robot is rated to provide an output of 5V, 1 A).

1. The first step in connecting the Raspberry Pi's 5V GPIO power supply is soldering a red and black piece of wire (of appropriate length) from the 5V and GND pins, respectively (as shown in the figure here):

Solder red and black pieces of wires from 5V and GND pins

2. Now, connect the red and black wires to terminal marked **5-12V motor** power (Red wire goes to + and Black wire goes to -).

Connect 5V and GND to the motor power supply terminals

3. Now, power up your Raspberry Pi Zero and measure the voltage across your motor power supply terminals. It should be receiving 5V, and the power LED of the motor driver should be glowing green (as shown in the next picture). If not, check the solder connections of the motor driver.

Green LED lights up when the Raspberry Pi Zero is powered up

4. This method is useful only when low-power motors are used (like the ones used in this chapter). If you have a motor with a higher voltage rating (voltage rating greater than 5V), you need to connect an external power supply. We will review connecting an external power supply in the next section.

If you find your Raspberry Pi Zero constantly resetting itself while driving your robot, it is possible that the USB battery pack is not able to drive the robot's motors. It is time to connect an external power supply!

# Using an external power supply

In this section, we are going to discuss connecting an external power supply to drive the motors. We will discuss connecting a 6V power supply to power the motors.

1. We will make use of a battery pack that consists of 4 AA batteries to drive the motors (battery packs available at http://a.co/hVPxfzD).
2. We need to install the battery pack such that it leads could be connected to the motor drivers power terminals.
3. The robot chassis kit came with an additional aluminum plate that could be used to install the battery pack (shown in the figure here):

Additional aluminium plate to hold the battery pack

4. We made use of four M2.5 stand-offs (shown in the picture) to hold the aluminum plate:

Assemble M2.5 stand-offs to hold the aluminium plate

5. Now, we used M2.5 screws to secure the aluminum plate (as shown in the figure here):

Secure the aluminium plate

6. Using double-sided tape, the battery pack was installed (the battery pack contains four AA batteries) on top of the aluminum plate. Then, the red and black wires of the battery pack are connected to the + and - terminals of the motor driver, respectively (as shown in the figure here).

Battery installed on the aluminium plate

7. Slide the battery pack switch to **ON**, and the motor driver should turn on as explained in the previous section.

Thus, the power supply setup is complete. In the next section, we will discuss taking the robot on a test drive.

 If you are looking for a battery with a higher capacity for your robot, we recommend considering LiPo batteries. This also means that you need motors with a better rating and a chassis that can withstand the battery weight.

# Testing the motors

In this section, we will verify that the motor driver is detected by the Raspberry Pi Zero and test the motor function. In the test, we will verify that the motors are rotating in the same direction.

# Motor driver detection

In this section, we will verify that the motor driver is detected by the Raspberry Pi Zero. The Raspberry Pi Zero *talks* to the motor driver via the I²C interface (Refer to `Chapter 4,` *Communication Interfaces*, if you are not familiar with the I²C interface). Hence, we need to enable the I²C interface of the Raspberry Pi Zero. There are two ways to enable the I²C interface:

**Method 1: From the Desktop**

Like enabling `ssh` by launching the Raspberry Pi Configuration from your Raspberry Pi Zero's desktop, you can enable the I²C interface from the interface tab of the configuration (shown in the snapshot here):

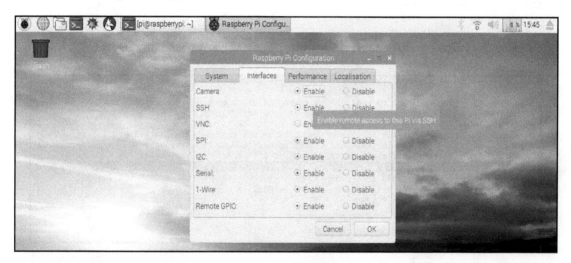

Enable I²C interface

**Method 2: From the command line**

We strongly recommend using this method as a practice toward getting comfortable with the command-line interface on the Raspberry Pi and remote login via `ssh`.

1. Log in to your Raspberry Pi Zero via `ssh` (Refer to `Chapter 11,` *Tips and Tricks*, for a tutorial on the `ssh` access).

2. Upon login, launch `raspi-config` as follows:

   ```
   sudo raspi-config.
   ```

3. It should launch the config options menu (shown in the screenshot here):

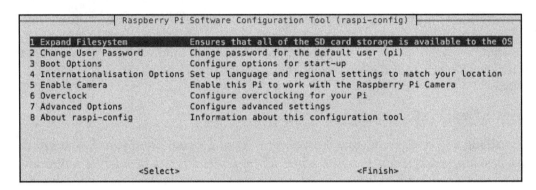

The raspi-config menu

4. Select **Option 7: Advanced Options** (using the keyboard) and select **A7: I2C**

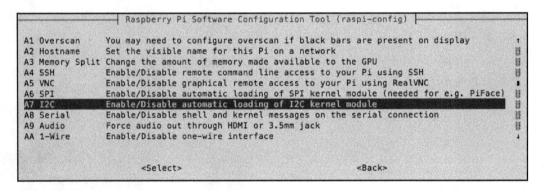

Select the I²C interface

5. Select **Yes** to enable the I²C interface.

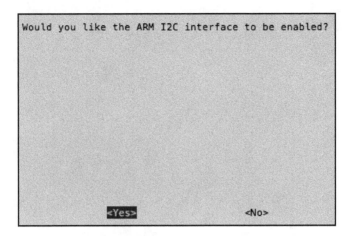

Would you like the ARM I2C interface to be enabled?

<Yes>          <No>

Enable the I$^2$C interface

6. Now that the I$^2$C interface is enabled, let's get started with detecting the motor driver.

# Detecting motor driver

The motor driver is connected to I$^2$C port-1 (the I$^2$C port-0 serves a different purpose. Refer to Chapter 11, *Tips and Tricks*, for more information). We will make use of the i2cdetect command to scan for devices connected via the I$^2$C interface. On your command-line interface, run the following command:

```
sudo i2cdetect -y 1
```

It provides an output that looks like this:

0

1

2

3

4

5

6

```
7

8

9

a

b

c

d

e

f

00:

-- -- -- -- -- -- -- -- -- -- -- -- --

10: -- -- -- -- -- -- -- -- -- -- -- -- -- -- -- --

20: -- -- -- -- -- -- -- -- -- -- -- -- -- -- -- --

30: -- -- -- -- -- -- -- -- -- -- -- -- -- -- -- --

40: -- -- -- -- -- -- -- -- -- -- -- -- -- -- --

50: -- -- -- -- -- -- -- -- -- -- -- -- -- -- -- --

60: 60 -- -- -- -- -- -- -- -- -- -- -- -- -- -- --

70: 70 -- -- -- -- -- -- --
```

I²C chips come with a 7-bit address that is used to identify the chip and establish communication. In this case, the I²C interface address is `0x60` (refer to the motor driver documentation at https://learn.adafruit.com/adafruit-dc-and-stepper-motor-hat-for-raspberry-pi). As shown in the output earlier, the Raspberry Pi Zero detects the motor driver. It is time to test if we can control the motors.

# Motor test

In this section, we are going to test the motors; that is, determine if we can drive the motors using the motor driver. In this test, we determined if the Raspberry Pi's supply was sufficient to drive the motors (or whether an external battery pack) was necessary.

In order to get started, we need to install the motor driver libraries (distributed by Adafruit under MIT license) and its dependency packages.

# Dependencies

The dependencies for the motor driver libraries may be installed from the command-line terminal of your Raspberry Pi Zero as follows (you may skip this step if you installed these tools while working on `Chapter 4`, *Communication Interfaces*):

```
sudo apt-get update
sudo apt-get install python3-dev python3-smbus
```

The next step is cloning the motor driver library:

```
git clone https://github.com/sai-y/Adafruit-Motor-HAT-Python-
Library.git
```

This library is a fork of the *Adafruit Motor HAT library*. We fixed some issues to make the library installation compatible with Python 3.x.

The library can be installed as follows:

```
cd Adafruit-Motor-HAT-Python-Library
sudo python3 setup.py install
```

Now that the libraries are installed, let's write a program that rotates the motors continuously:

1. As always, the first step is importing the `MotorHAT` module:

   ```
   from Adafruit_MotorHAT import Adafruit_MotorHAT,
   Adafruit_DCMotor
   ```

2. The next step is to create an instance of the `MotorHAT` class and establish the interface with the motor driver (as discussed in the previous section, the motor driver's 7-bit address is `0x60`).

3. The motors of the robot are connected to channels 1 and 2. Hence, we need to initialize two instances of the `Adafruit_DCMotor` class that represent the left and right motors of the robot:

   ```
   left_motor = motor_driver.getMotor(1)
   right_motor = motor_driver.getMotor(2)
   ```

4. The next step is setting the motor speed and motor direction. The motor speed can be set using an integer between `0` and `255` (which corresponds to 0% and 100% of the motor's rated rpm). Let's set the motor speed at 100%:

   ```
   left_motor.setSpeed(255)
   right_motor.setSpeed(255)
   ```

5. Let's rotate the motors in the forward direction:

   ```
   left_motor.run(Adafruit_MotorHAT.FORWARD)
   right_motor.run(Adafruit_MotorHAT.FORWARD)
   ```

6. Let's rotate both the motors in the forward direction for 5 seconds and then reduce the speed:

   ```
   left_motor.setSpeed(200)
   right_motor.setSpeed(200)
   ```

7. Now, let's rotate the motors in the reverse direction:

   ```
   left_motor.run(Adafruit_MotorHAT.BACKWARD)
   right_motor.run(Adafruit_MotorHAT.BACKWARD)
   ```

8. Let's turn off the motors once we are done rotating the motors in the reverse direction for 5 seconds:

   ```
   left_motor.run(Adafruit_MotorHAT.RELEASE)
   ```

```
    right_motor.run(Adafruit_MotorHAT.RELEASE)
```

Putting it altogether:

```
from Adafruit_MotorHAT import Adafruit_MotorHAT, Adafruit_DCMotor
from time import sleep


if __name__ == "__main__":
  motor_driver = Adafruit_MotorHAT(addr=0x60)

  left_motor = motor_driver.getMotor(1)
  right_motor = motor_driver.getMotor(2)

  left_motor.setSpeed(255)
  right_motor.setSpeed(255)

  left_motor.run(Adafruit_MotorHAT.FORWARD)
  right_motor.run(Adafruit_MotorHAT.FORWARD)

  sleep(5)

  left_motor.setSpeed(200)
  right_motor.setSpeed(200)

  left_motor.run(Adafruit_MotorHAT.BACKWARD)
  right_motor.run(Adafruit_MotorHAT.BACKWARD)

  sleep(5)

  left_motor.run(Adafruit_MotorHAT.RELEASE)
  right_motor.run(Adafruit_MotorHAT.RELEASE)
```

The preceding code sample is available for download along with this chapter as
`motor_test.py`. Recharge the USB battery pack before you test the motors. We picked the
test duration long enough to verify the motor direction, performance, and so on.

 If your Raspberry Pi Zero seems to be resetting itself while running or the
motors aren't running at the rated speed, it is an indicator that the motors
are not being driven with the sufficient current. Switch over to a power
source that meets the requirement (this may involve switching from the
GPIO's power supply to the battery pack or switching to a battery pack of
higher capacity).

Now that the motors are tested, let us set up a camera for the robot.

# Camera setup

 You will need a Raspberry Pi Zero 1.3 or higher to set up the camera. We discussed identifying your Raspberry Pi Zero's board version at the beginning of this chapter. You may also skip this section if you are familiar with setting up the camera from `Chapter 8`, *Awesome Things You Could Develop Using Python*.

In this section, we will set up the camera for the robot. The Raspberry Pi Zero (v1.3 onward) comes with a camera adapter. This enables adding a camera module to the robot (designed and manufactured by the Raspberry Pi foundation). The camera module was designed to suit different models of the Raspberry Pi.

The Raspberry Pi Zero's camera interface needs an adapter that is different than the ones meant for other models. The sources to purchase the camera and the adapter were shared with the bill of materials of this chapter.

Let's get started:

1. Ensure that your Raspberry Pi Zero is powered down and identify the shorter side of the camera adapter. In the image shown here, the shorter side is to the right.

Pi Zero Camera Adapter-Image source: adafruit.com

2. Carefully, slide out the camera interface of the Raspberry Pi zero (as shown in the picture here). Pay attention to avoid breaking your camera interface tab.

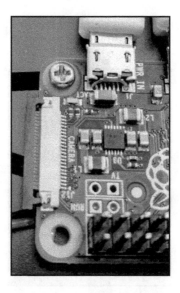

Slide the tabs of the camera interface carefully

3. Gently slide in the camera module. Latch the camera adapter cable and gently tug on it to make sure that the adapter cable doesn't slide out of its position. The camera adapter should be seated, as shown in the picture here.

Camera adapter placement

4.  Repeat the exercise for the other end of the camera adapter to interface it with the camera module.

Insert adapter on the other side

5.  The camera adapter cable can be unwieldy while trying to install the camera on the robot. We recommend installing a mount (source shared in the bill of materials).

Raspberry Pi camera module mount

6.  Using the double-sided tape, install the camera to the front of your robot.

Camera mounted in front of the robot

7. Log in to your Raspberry Pi Zero's desktop via ssh to enable and test the camera interface.

8. Enabling the camera interface is similar to enabling the I²C interface discussed earlier in this chapter. Launch Raspberry Pi configuration using the raspi-config command:

```
sudo raspi-config
```

Select **Option P1: Enable Camera** (found under **Interfacing Options** of the main configuration menu) and enable the camera:

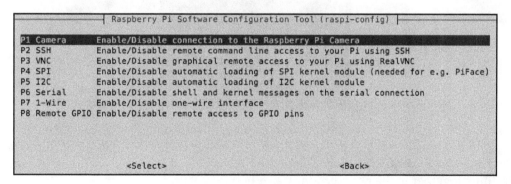

The screenshot of the Raspberry Configuration screen

9. Reboot your Raspberry Pi Zero!

# Verification of camera function

1. Once your reboot is complete, run the following command from the Command Prompt:

   ```
   raspistill -o test_picture
   ```

2. Since your robot is completely assembled, the HDMI port of your Raspberry Pi Zero is probably inaccessible. You should retrieve the file using the `scp` command.

    On a Windows Machine, you can copy files from your Raspberry Pi Zero using a tool such as WinSCP. On a Mac/Linux desktop, you can use the `scp` command. Refer to `Chapter 11`, *Tips and Tricks*, for a detailed tutorial on remote login and copying of files from your Raspberry Pi Zero.

   ```
   scp pi@192.168.86.111:/home/pi/test_output .
   ```

3. Examine the picture taken using the Raspberry Pi camera module to verify its function

Picture of a coffee cup taken using the Raspberry Pi camera module

Now that we have verified the function of the robot's components, we are going to bring everything together in the next section.

# The web interface

Our objective behind building this robot as one of our final projects is to demonstrate using the topics discussed in this book in application development. To that end, we are going to make use of object-oriented programming and web frameworks to build a web interface to control the robot.

In `Chapter 7`, *Requests and Web Frameworks*, we discussed the `flask` web framework. We are going to make use of `flask` to stream a live view of the camera module to a browser. We are also going to add buttons to the web interface that enables steering the robot. Let's get started!

 Refer to `Chapter 7`, *Requests and Web Frameworks*, for installation instructions and a basic tutorial on the `flask` framework.

Let's get started by implementing a simple web interface where we add four buttons to control the robot in the forward, reverse, left, and right directions. Let's assume that the robot moves at maximum speed in all directions.

We are going to make use of object-oriented programming to implement the motor control. We are going to demonstrate the use of object-oriented programming to simplify things (this concept of simplification is known as **abstraction**). Let's implement a `Robot` class that implements the motor control. This `Robot` class would initialize the motor driver and handle all control functions of the robot.

1. Open a file named `robot.py` to implement the `Robot` class.
2. In order to control the movement of the robot, the robot needs the motor driver channels that are being used (to drive the motors) as inputs during initialization.
3. Hence, the `__init__()` function of the `Robot` class would be something as follows:

```
import time
from Adafruit_MotorHAT import Adafruit_MotorHAT


class Robot(object):
  def __init__(self, left_channel, right_channel):
    self.motor = Adafruit_MotorHAT(0x60)
    self.left_motor = self.motor.getMotor(left_channel)
    self.right_motor = self.motor.getMotor(right_channel)
```

4. In the preceding code snippet, the __init__() function requires the channels being used to connect the left and right motors to the motor driver board as arguments.

5. When an instance of the Robot class is created, the motor driver (Adafruit_MotorHAT) is initialized and the motor channels are initialized.

6. Let's write methods to move the robot in the forward and reverse directions:

```
def forward(self, duration):
    self.set_speed()
    self.left_motor.run(Adafruit_MotorHAT.FORWARD)
    self.right_motor.run(Adafruit_MotorHAT.FORWARD)
    time.sleep(duration)
    self.stop()

def reverse(self, duration):
    self.set_speed()
    self.left_motor.run(Adafruit_MotorHAT.BACKWARD)
    self.right_motor.run(Adafruit_MotorHAT.BACKWARD)
    time.sleep(duration)
    self.stop()
```

7. Let's also write methods to move the robot in left- and right-hand side directions. In order to turn the robot left, we need to turn the left motor off and keep the right motor on and vice versa. This creates a turning moment and turns the robot in that direction:

```
def left(self, duration):
    self.set_speed()
    self.right_motor.run(Adafruit_MotorHAT.FORWARD)
    time.sleep(duration)
    self.stop()

def right(self, duration):
    self.set_speed()
    self.left_motor.run(Adafruit_MotorHAT.FORWARD)
    time.sleep(duration)
    self.stop()
```

8. Thus, we have implemented a Robot class that drives the robot in the four directions. Let's implement a simple test so that we can test the Robot class before we use it in our main program:

```
if __name__ == "__main__":
    # create an instance  of the robot class with channels 1 and 2
    robot = Robot(1,2)
```

```
print("Moving forward...")
robot.forward(5)
print("Moving backward...")
robot.reverse(5)
robot.stop()
```

The preceding code sample is available for download along with this chapter as `robot.py`. Try to run the program with the motor driver. It should run the motor in forward and reverse directions for 5 seconds. Now that we have implemented a stand-alone module for the robot's control, let's move on to the web interface.

# Camera setup for the web interface

 You will encounter some issues even after following the instructions to the tee. We have included references that we used to fix the problem at the end of this chapter.

In this section, we will set up the camera to stream to a browser. The first step is installing the `motion` package:

```
sudo apt-get install motion
```

Once the package is installed, the following configuration changes need to be applied:

1. Edit the following parameters in `/etc/motion/motion.conf`:

```
daemon on
threshold 99999
framerate 90
stream_maxrate 100
stream_localhost off
```

2. Include the following parameter in `/etc/default/motion`:

```
start_motion_daemon=yes
```

3. Edit `/etc/init.d/motion` as follows:

```
start)

if check_daemon_enabled ; then

if ! [ -d /var/run/motion ]; then
```

```
mkdir /var/run/motion

fi

chown motion:motion /var/run/motion

sudo modprobe bcm2835-v4l2

chmod 777 /var/run/motion

sleep 30

log_daemon_msg "Starting $DESC" "$NAME"
```

4. Reboot your Raspberry Pi Zero.
5. The next step assumes that you have installed the flask framework and tried out the basic example from `Chapter 7`, *Requests and Web Frameworks*.
6. Create a folder named `templates` within the folder where your `flask` framework and
   `Robot` class files are located) and create a file named `index.html` in the folder with the following contents:

```html
<!DOCTYPE html>
  <html>
    <head>
      <title>Raspberry Pi Zero Robot</title>
    </head>

    <body>
     <iframe id="stream"
     src="http://<IP_Address_of_your_Raspberry_Pi>
     :8081/?action=stream" width="320" height="240">
     </iframe>
    </body>
  </html>
```

7. In the preceding code snippet, include the IP address of your Raspberry Pi Zero and save it as `index.html`.

8. Create a file named `web_interface.py` and serve `index.html` saved to the templates folder:

```
from flask import Flask, render_template
app = Flask(__name__)

@app.route("/")
def hello():
    return render_template('index.html')

if __name__ == "__main__":
    app.run('0.0.0.0')
```

9. Run the flask server using the following command:

**python3 web_interface.py**

10. Open a browser on your laptop and go to the IP address of your Raspberry Pi Zero (port 5000) to see a live stream of your Raspberry Pi cam module.

The snapshot of the live webcam stream (Raspberry Pi Cam module)

Let's move on to the next step to add buttons to the web interface.

# Buttons for robot control

In this section, we will add implement buttons to the web interface to drive the robot.

1. The first step is adding four buttons to `index.html`. We will be making use of HTML Table to add four buttons (Code snippet shortened for brevity and refer to `http://www.w3schools.com/html/html_tables.asp` for more information on HTML tables):

```html
<table style="width:100%; max-width: 500px; height:300px;">
  <tr>
    <td>
      <form action="/forward" method="POST">
        <input type="submit" value="forward" style="float:
        left; width:80% ;">
        </br>
      </form>
    </td>
  ...
</table>
```

2. In `web_interface.py`, we need to implement a method that accepts `POST` requests from the buttons. For example, the method to accept requests from `/forward` can be implemented as follows:

```python
@app.route('/forward', methods = ['POST'])
def forward():
    my_robot.forward(0.25)
    return redirect('/')
```

3. Putting it altogether, `web_interface.py` looks something as follows:

```python
from flask import Flask, render_template, request, redirect
from robot import Robot

app = Flask(__name__)
my_robot = Robot(1,2)

@app.route("/")
def hello():
    return render_template('index.html')

@app.route('/forward', methods = ['POST'])
def forward():
    my_robot.forward(0.25)
    return redirect('/')
```

```
@app.route('/reverse', methods = ['POST'])
def reverse():
    my_robot.reverse(0.25)
    return redirect('/')

@app.route('/left', methods = ['POST'])
def left():
    my_robot.left(0.25)
    return redirect('/')

@app.route('/right', methods = ['POST'])
def right():
    my_robot.right(0.25)
    return redirect('/')

if __name__ == "__main__":
    app.run('0.0.0.0')
```

The preceding code sample is available for download along with this chapter as
web_interface.py (along with index.html). Add the following line to
/etc/rc.local(before exit 0):

**python3 /<path_to_webserver_file>/web_interface.py**

Reboot your Raspberry Pi Zero, and you should see a live feed of the robot's camera. You
should also be able to control the robot from the browser!

Control your robot a browser!

# Troubleshooting tips

Here are some of the problems we encountered while building the robot:

- We broke our Raspberry Pi Zero's camera interface tab while assembling the camera module. We had to replace the Raspberry Pi Zero.
- We encountered some ghost issues with our motor drive circuitry. We were not able to detect the motor driver on certain occasions. We had to replace the power supply for the motor driver. We will keep this book's website updated when we find the root cause of this issue.
- We encountered a lot of issues getting the web stream setup for the browser. We had to tweak a lot of settings to get it working. We found some articles to fix the issue. We have shared them in the references section of this book.

# Project enhancements

- Consider making enhancements to the web interface such that you could alter the speed of your robot.
- If you are planning to build a robot that operates in outdoor conditions, you potentially add a GPS sensor. Most GPS sensors stream data via the UART interface. We recommend reading Chapter 4, *Communication Interfaces* for examples.
- The distance of obstacles can be measured using this sensor: `https://www.adafruit.com/products/3317`. This can be helpful in telemetry applications.
- * In this book, we used a camera to drive the robot. It is possible to take pictures and understand the objects in a scene using this image understanding tool: `https://cloud.google.com/vision/`.

# Summary

In this chapter, we built a robot that consists of a pair of motors driven by a Raspberry Pi using a motor driver. The robot is also equipped with a camera module to aid steering the robot. It consists of two battery packs to power the Raspberry Pi Zero and motors, respectively. We will also upload a video of the robot's operation to this book's website.

**Learning resources**

- *Differential steering mechanism*:
  https://www.robotix.in/tutorial/mechanical/drivemechtut/
- *Video lecture on differential steering mechanism*:
  https://www.coursera.org/learn/mobile-robot/lecture/GnbnD/differential-drive-robots
- *Make Magazine: Building your own chassis*:
  https://makezine.com/projects/designing-a-robot-chassis/
- *Society of robots: Guide to building your own chassis*:
  http://www.societyofrobots.com/mechanics_chassisconstruction.shtml
- *Adafruit's motor driver documentation*:
  https://learn.adafruit.com/adafruit-dc-and-stepper-motor-hat-for-raspberry-pi
- *Adafruit motor selection guide*:
  https://learn.adafruit.com/adafruit-motor-selection-guide
- *Adafruit's guide on building a simple Raspberry Pi based robot*:https://learn.adafruit.com/simple-raspberry-pi-robot/overview
- *Flask framework and form submission*:http://opentechschool.github.io/python-flask/core/form-submission.html
- *Raspberry Pi Camera Setup for web streaming*:
  http://jamespoole.me/2016/04/29/web-controlled-robot-with-video-stream/

# 10
# Home Automation Using the Raspberry Pi Zero

As the title of the chapter suggests, we will discuss home improvement projects involving the Raspberry Pi Zero in this chapter. We selected our projects such that each example could be executed as a weekend project.

The projects include the following topics:

- Voice-activated personal assistant
- Web framework-based appliance control
- Physical activity motivation tool
- Smart lawn sprinkler

## Voice activated personal assistant

In our first project, we are going to emulate personal assistants such as Google Home (https://madeby.google.com/home/) and Amazon Echo (http://a.co/cQ6zJk6) using a Raspberry Pi Zero. We will build an application where we can add reminders and events to a calendar and controlling appliances.

We will be making use of **houndify** (houndify.com)—a tool that is designed to provide interactions with smart devices. We will install the requisite software tools on the Raspberry Pi Zero. We will interface a button to the Raspberry Pi Zero's GPIO. We will write some code to create reminders and turn on/off appliances using *Houndify*.

The following accessories (apart from your Raspberry Pi Zero) are recommended for this project:

| Item | Source | Price (in USD) |
|---|---|---|
| USB sound card | `http://a.co/824dfM8` | 8.79 |
| Microphone amplifier board with adjustable gain | `https://www.adafruit.com/products/1713` | 7.95 |
| 3.5 mm auxiliary cable | `https://www.adafruit.com/products/2698` | 2.50 |
| Momentary push button set | `https://www.adafruit.com/products/1009` | 5.95 |
| Breadboard, resistors, jumper wires, and capacitors | N. A. | N. A. |
| Speaker (suggestion) | `http://a.co/3h9uaTI` | 14.99 |

# Installing requisite packages

The first step is installing the requisite packages for the project. This includes the following packages: `python3-pyaudio python3-numpy`. They may be installed as follows:

```
sudo apt-get update
sudo apt-get install alsa-utils mplayer python3-numpy
```

# How does it work?

The following are the steps to be performed:

1. A push button is interfaced to the Raspberry Pi Zero's GPIO. When the GPIO button is pressed, the recorder is turned on (at the start of a beep sound from the speaker).
2. The recorder accepts the user request and processes it using the `Houndify` library.
3. The assistant processes the audio file using `Houndify` and responds to the user request.

In this project, we are using a push button to start listening to user requests, whereas commercially available products, such as Amazon's Echo or the Google Home, have special hardware (along with software) to enable this capability. We are using a push button to simplify the problem.

# Setting up the audio tools

In this section, we will connect the USB sound card, speaker, and the microphone for the project.

## Connecting the speaker

Perform the following steps to connect to speakers:

1. Connect the USB sound card to your Raspberry Pi Zero and find out if the USB sound card enumerates using the `lsusb` command (on your Raspberry Pi Zero's command-line terminal):

```
[pi@raspberrypi:~ $ lsusb
Bus 001 Device 006: ID 093a:2510 Pixart Imaging, Inc. Optical Mouse
Bus 001 Device 005: ID 0d8c:000c C-Media Electronics, Inc. Audio Adapter
Bus 001 Device 004: ID 045e:00dd Microsoft Corp. Comfort Curve Keyboard 2000 V1.0
Bus 001 Device 003: ID 0bda:8176 Realtek Semiconductor Corp. RTL8188CUS 802.11n WLAN Adapter
Bus 001 Device 002: ID 1a40:0101 Terminus Technology Inc. 4-Port HUB
Bus 001 Device 001: ID 1d6b:0002 Linux Foundation 2.0 root hub
```

USB sound card enumeration

2. Cheap USB sound cards typically have an input terminal (to connect a microphone) and an output terminal (to connect a speaker). Both the terminals are standard 3.5 mm jacks. The input terminal is pink and typically marked with a microphone symbol. The output terminal is green and marked with a speaker symbol.
3. Connect a speaker to the output terminal (green) of the USB sound card.
4. On your Raspberry Pi Zero's command-line terminal, list all the audio sources connected to your Raspberry Pi Zero using the following command:

```
aplay -l
**** List of PLAYBACK Hardware Devices ****
card 0: ALSA [bcm2835 ALSA], device 0: bcm2835
  ALSA [bcm2835 ALSA]
Subdevices: 8/8
Subdevice #0: subdevice #0
```

```
Subdevice #1: subdevice #1
Subdevice #2: subdevice #2
Subdevice #3: subdevice #3
Subdevice #4: subdevice #4
Subdevice #5: subdevice #5
Subdevice #6: subdevice #6
Subdevice #7: subdevice #7
card 0: ALSA [bcm2835 ALSA], device 1: bcm2835
  ALSA [bcm2835 IEC958/HDMI]
Subdevices: 1/1
Subdevice #0: subdevice #0
card 1: Set [C-Media USB Headphone Set],
  device 0: USB Audio [USB Audio]
Subdevices: 1/1
Subdevice #0: subdevice #0
```

5. As shown in the `aplay` command's output, the sound card is listed as `card 1`. We need this information to set the USB sound card as the default audio source

6. Open your sound configuration file from the command line as follows:

   `nano ~/.asoundrc`

7. Make sure that the configuration file's source is set to `card 1` (the soundcard):

   ```
   pcm.!default {
           type hw
           card 1
   }

   ctl.!default {
           type hw
           card 1
   }
   ```

   Save the configuration file (by pressing *Ctrl+X* and press *Y* to confirm the name of the file. Press *Enter* to save the file. Refer to `Chapter 11`, *Tips and Tricks* chapter for a detailed tutorial) and reboot your Raspberry Pi Zero.

8. On reboot, test if the speaker works by downloading a wave file (`Freesound.org` has plenty of wave files). From the command-line terminal, play your file as follows:

   `aplay test.wav`

If everything is configured properly, you should be able to play audio using your USB sound card and speaker. If you are not able to play the audio, check the connections and make sure that your USB sound card is enumerated correctly and you have chosen the right audio source in the configuration file. In the next section, we will set up the microphone.

# Connecting the microphone

In this section, we will be setting up an omnidirectional microphone to listen for commands/inputs.

 We tested off-the-shelf electret microphones, and the audio quality was not sufficient to perform speech recognition on the recorded audio samples. As an alternative, we recommend boundary microphones for a wide pickup, for example, `http://a.co/8YKSy4c`.

MAX9814 with omnidirectional microphone Source: Adafruit.com

1. The gain of the amplifier can be set to three levels: **60 dB** when the gain pin is unconnected, **50 dB** when the gain pin is connected to ground, and **40 dB** when the gain pin is connected to $V_{dd}$.

2. Connect **Vdd** and the **GND** pins to the **5V** and **GND** pins of the Raspberry Pi's GPIO pins (,pins 4 and 6 of the Raspberry Pi's GPIO).

3. Cut the 3.5 mm cable into two halves. It consists of three wires connected to the **Tip**, **Ring** and **Sleeve** of the 3.5 mm connector (as shown in the picture here). Use a multimeter to identify the **Sleeve**, **Tip**, and **Ring** wires of the 3.5 mm connector.

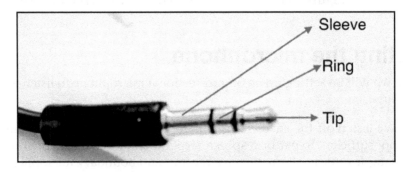

Cut the auxiliary cable and identify the three wires of the cable

4. Connect a 100 mF electrolytic capacitor to the output of the amplifier where the positive lead is connected to the output and the other end is connected to the tip of the 3.5 mm connector. The ground pin of the amplifier is connected to the sleeve of the 3.5 mm connector.

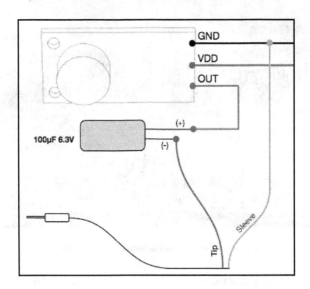

Microphone connections to the 3.5 mm connector

The microphone is ready to use. Power the microphone using the GPIO pins of the Raspberry Pi Zero and plug the 3.5 mm connector into the input terminals of the USB sound card (marked with the microphone symbol).

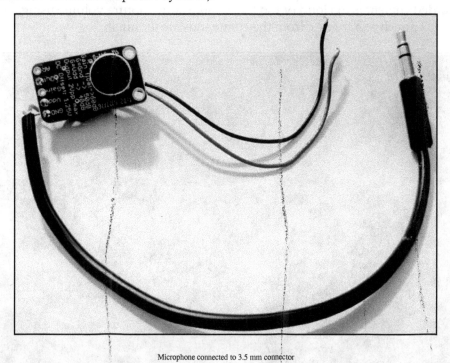

Microphone connected to 3.5 mm connector

We are ready to test the microphone and set an optimal capture volume. From the Raspberry Pi Zero's command-line terminal, run the following command:

```
arecord -f dat -D plughw:2
    --duration=10~/home/pi/rectest.wav
```

This will record the file for 10 seconds. Play it back using the `aplay` command:

```
aplay rectest.wav
```

You should be able to hear the recorded conversation. Check your connections whether you don't hear anything (**GND**, **5V**, amplifier output pins, and so on. We have also included additional resources for the microphone troubleshooting at the end of this chapter). If the recorded content is too loud or too feeble, adjust the capture volume using `alsamixer`. Launch `alsamixer` from the command-line terminal:

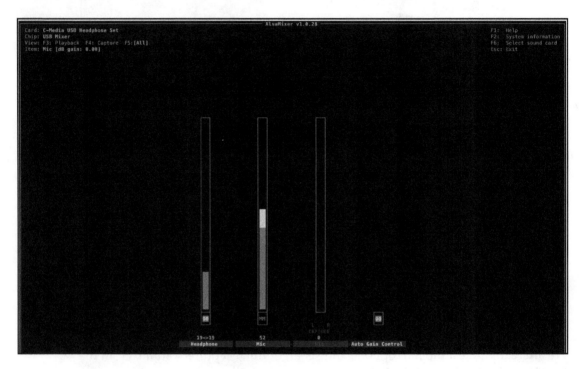

alsamixer control panel

Press *F5* to view all options. Use the arrow keys to adjust the value and M to disable autogain control. Let's move on to the next section where we build our application.

# Houndify

**Houndify** (www.houndify.com) is a tool that enables adding voice interaction to devices. Their free account enables performing 44 different types of actions. Sign up for an account on their website and activate it (via your e-mail).

1. Once your account is activated, go to your account dashboard to create a new client:

 On creating a new account, a new client is automatically created. This client may not work properly. Delete it and create a new client from the dashboard.

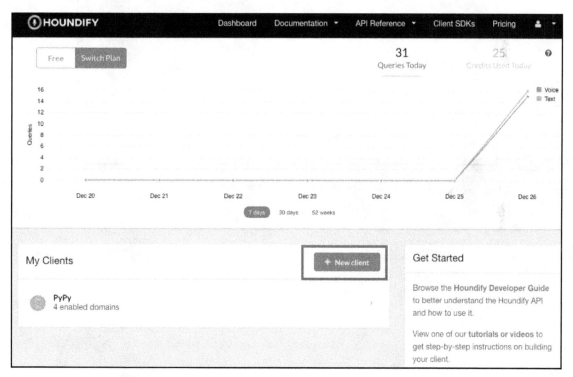

Create new client

2. Give a name to your application and select the platform to be **Home Automation**.

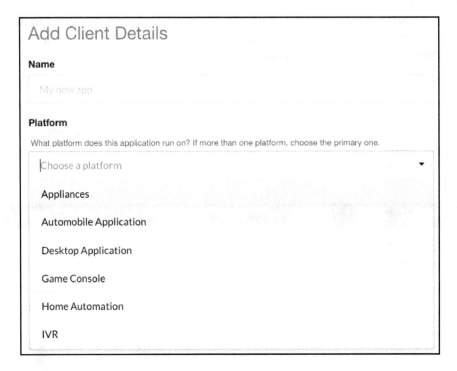

Name the application and select the platform

3. The next step is selecting domains, that is, the nature of applications the assistant must support. Select **Weather**, **Stock Market**, **Dictionary**, and so on.

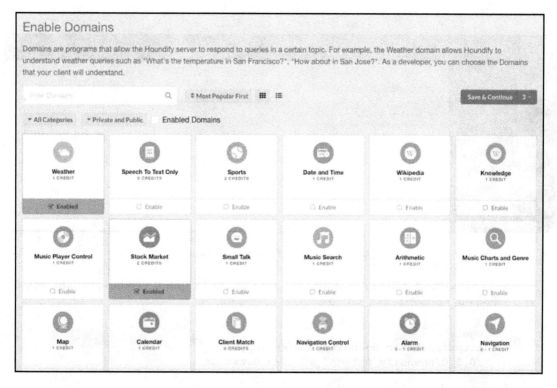

Enable domains

4. Click on **Save & Continue**. Once you have created your new client, click on it (from the dashboard) to retrieve the following credentials: **Client ID** and **Client Key**.

Copy the Client id and the Client Key from the dashboard

5. We also need to download the SDK for Python 3.x (latest version available at `https://docs.houndify.com/sdks#python`):

```
wget
https://static.houndify.com/sdks/python
/0.5.0/houndify_python3_sdk_0.5.0.tar.gz
```

6. Extract the package as follows:

```
tar -xvzf houndify_python3_sdk_0.5.0.tar.gzrm
houndify_python3_sdk_0.5.0.tar.gz
```

7. The SDK comes with plenty of examples to get started. Let's consider a scenario where you would like to find out the weather at your current location by interacting with the voice assistant:

1. Get your current GPS coordinates from a tool such as Google Maps. For example, the GPS coordinates for a specific intersection in San Francisco, California is 37.778724, -122.414778. Let's try to find the weather at this specific location.

2. Open the `sample_wave.py` file and modify `line 39` of the file:

```
client.setLocation(37.778724, -37.778724)
```

3. Save the file and from the command-line terminal, change directories to the `Houndify SDK folder`:

```
cd houndify_python3_sdk_0.5.0/
./sample_wave.py <client_id> <client_key>
test_audio/whatistheweatherthere_nb.wav
```

4. After processing the request, it should print a detailed response:

```
src="//static.midomi.com/corpus/H_Zk82fGHFX/build/js/
templates.min.js"></script>'}}, 'TemplateName':
'VerticalTemplateList', 'AutoListen': False,
'WeatherCommandKind': 'ShowWeatherCurrentConditions',
'SpokenResponseLong': 'The weather is 45 degrees and
mostly clear in San Francisco.',
```

We verified the function and setup of the Houndify SDK by testing the example. We uploaded an audio file to the Houndify server requesting the current weather information (play the audio file and find out). The `sample_wave.py` script takes the `client_id`, `client_key`, and the audio file as inputs. It prints out the output from the Houndify server.

 You need to enable specific domains to retrieve specific information. For example, we enabled the weather domain to retrieve the weather information. It is also possible to add custom commands to the program.

In the next section, we will modify `sample_wave.py` to build our application.

# Building voice commands

Let's get started with building our voice assistant that we can use to find the weather and turn on/off lights. Because we enabled the weather domain while setting up our Houndify account, we need to add custom commands to turn on/off lights:

1. On your Houndify dashboard, go to your client's home page. **Dashboard | Click on your client**.
2. Locate **Custom Commands** on the navigation bar to the left. Let's add a custom command each to turn on and turn off the light.

3. Delete `ClientMatch #1` that comes as a template with the custom commands.

Locate Custom commands and Delete Client Match #1

4. Select **Add ClientMatch** to add a custom command to turn on lights. Populate the fields with the following information:

- **Expression**: `["Turn"].("Lights"). ["ON"]`
- **Result**: `{"action": "turn_light_on"}`
- **SpokenResponse**: `Turning Lights On`
- **SpokenResponseLong**: `Turning your Lights On`
- **WrittenResponse**: `Turning Lights On`
- **WrittenResponseLong**: `Turning your Lights On`

5. Repeat the preceding steps to add a command to turn lights off

Test and verify that these commands work using `sample_wave.py`. Make your own recording for the test. We have also provided audio files along with this chapter's download (available in the folder `audio_files`).

Let's make a copy of `sample_wave.py` to build our assistant. We recommend reading through the file and familiarizing yourself with its function. The detailed documentation for the Houndify SDK is available at `https://docs.houndify.com/sdks/docs/python`:

1. In the file `stream_wav.py`, the `StreamingHoundClient` class is used to send audio queries, such as request for weather information and commands to turn on/off lights.
2. The `MyListener` class inherits the `HoundListener` class (from the `houndify` SDK).
3. The `MyListener` class implements callback functions for three scenarios:

   - Partial Transcription (the `onPartialTranscript` method)
   - Complete Transcription (the `onFinalResponse` method)
   - Error State (the `onError` method)

4. We need to make use of action intents to turning on/off lights using voice command.
5. When we implemented the custom commands on the Houndify website, we added an action intent for each command. For example, the action intent for turning on the lights was:

   ```
   {
       "action": "turn_light_on"
   }
   ```

6. In order to turn on/off the lights based on the received action intent, we need to import the `OutputDevice` class from `gpiozero`:

   ```
   from gpiozero import OutputDevice
   ```

7. The GPIO pin that controls the light is initialized in the __init__ method of the MyListener class:

```
class MyListener(houndify.HoundListener):
    def __init__(self):
        self.light = OutputDevice(3)
```

8. On completing transcription, if an action intent is received, the lights are either turned on or turned off. It is implemented as follows:

```
def onFinalResponse(self, response):
    if "AllResults" in response:
        result = response["AllResults"][0]
        if result['CommandKind'] == "ClientMatchCommand":
            if result["Result"]["action"] == "turn_light_on":
                self.light.on()
            elif result["Result"]["action"] == "turn_light_off":
                self.light.off()
```

 response is a dictionary that consists of the parsed json response. Refer to the SDK documentation and try printing the response yourself to understand its structure.

9. We also need to announce the voice assistant's action while turning on/off lights. We explored different text-to-speech tools, and they sounded robotic when compared with off-the-shelf products such as the Google Home or Amazon Echo. We came across this script that makes use of the *Google Speech-to-Text engine* at http://elinux.org/RPi_Text_to_Speech_(Speech_Synthesis).

 Because the script makes use of Google's text-to-speech engine, it connects to the Internet to fetch the transcribed audio data.

1. Open a new shell script from the Raspberry Pi's command-line terminal:

   ```
   nano speech.sh
   ```

2. Paste the following contents:

   ```bash
   #!/bin/bash
   say() { local IFS=+;/usr/bin/mplayer
   -ao alsa -really-quiet -noconsolecontrols
   "http://translate.google.com/translate_tts?
   ie=UTF-8&client=tw-ob&q=$*&tl=En-us"; }
   say $*
   ```

3. Make the file executable:

   ```
   chmod u+x speech.sh
   ```

4. We are going to make use of this script to announce any actions by the assistant. Test it from the command line using the following code:

   ```
   ~/speech.sh "Hello, World!"
   ```

5. The system calls to announce the voice assistant actions are implemented as follows:

   ```
   if result["Result"]["action"] == "turn_light_on":
       self.light.on()
       os.system("~/speech.sh Turning Lights On")
   elif result["Result"]["action"] == "turn_light_off":
       self.light.off()
       os.system("~/speech.sh Turning Lights Off")
   ```

Let's test what we have built so far in this section. The preceding code snippets are available for download along with this chapter as `voice_assistant_inital.py`. Make it executable as follows:

```
chmod +x voice_assistant_initial.py
```

Test the program as follows (audio files are also available for download with this chapter):

```
./voice_assistant.py turn_lights_on.wav
```

# Adding a button

Let's add a button to our voice assistant. This momentary push button is connected to pin 2 (BCM numbering) and the LED is connected to pin 3.

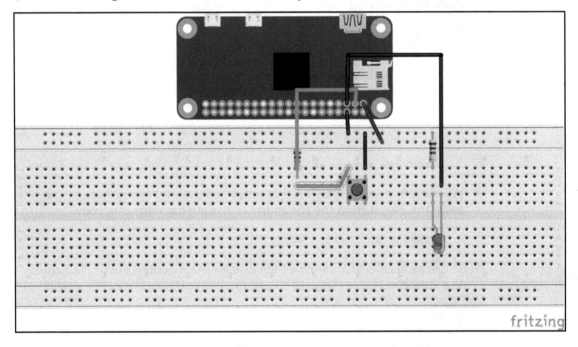

Voice Assistant interface setup

1. In order to read the button presses, we need to import the `Button` class from `gpiozero`:

   ```
   from gpiozero import Button, OutputDevice
   ```

2. When a button is pressed, the voice assistant needs to play a beep sound indicating that it is awaiting the user's command. Beep sounds of your choice can be downloaded from `www.freesound.org`.

3. Following the beep sound, the user command is recorded for a duration of 5 seconds. The recorded file is then processed using the *Houndify* SDK. The following code snippet shows the trigger function that is called when the button is pressed:

```
def trigger_function():
    os.system("aplay -D plughw:1,0 /home/pi/beep.wav")
    os.system("arecord -D plughw:2,0 -f S16_LE -d 5
    /home/pi/query.wav")
    os.system("aplay -D plughw:1,0 /home/pi/beep.wav")
    call_houndify()
```

4. The trigger function is registered as follows:

```
button = Button(4)
button.when_released = trigger_function
```

Connect the button and the LED to the Raspberry Pi's GPIO interface to test the voice assistant.

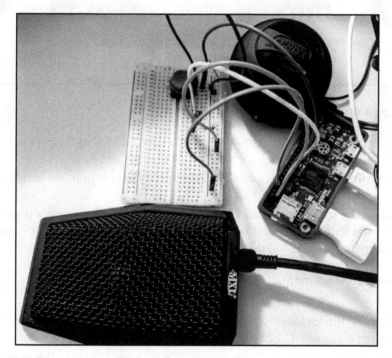

Voice assistant setup

The voice assistant code file is available for download along with this chapter as `voice_assistant.py`. Download the code sample and try the following commands:

```
What is the weather in San Francisco?What is the weather in Santa Clara,
California?Turn Lights OnTurn Lights Off
```

We have shared a video (on this book's site) that demonstrates the function of the voice assistant. Now, we have demonstrated the voice assistant using an LED. In order to control a table lamp, simply replace the LED with a power switch tail II (http://www.powerswitchtail.com/Pages/default.aspx).

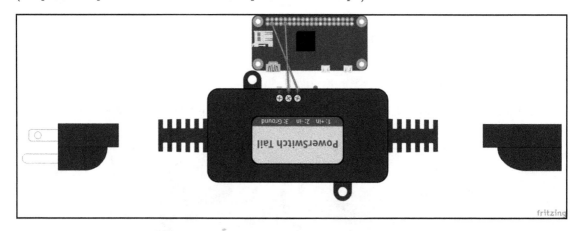

**Things to keep in mind:**

1. Add `voice_assistant.py` to `/etc/rc.local` so that it starts automatically on boot.
2. The entire setup can be unwieldy. Assemble the components inside an enclosure to organize the wiring.
3. Because the project involves electrical appliances, use prescribed cables and terminate them properly. Ensure that the cables are connected properly. We will share examples of the same on our website.

**Project ideas and enhancements:**

- Currently, the assistant works only at the press of a button. How will you make it listen for a keyword? For example, "Ok, Google" or "Alexa"?
- Is it possible to have a remote trigger? Think something on the lines of *Amazon Tap*.

- If you have lights such as Philips Hue or Internet-connected switches such as WeMo switch smartplug or the TP-Link Smart switch, you can control them using a voice assistant. IFTTT provides applets to control them yourself. Create a maker channel web hook to control them. Refer to Chapter 8 for examples.

# Web Framework based appliance control/dashboard

In this section, we will review building a dashboard in order to control appliances. This could be a dashboard for the aquarium where you would like to monitor all the requisite parameters for the tank or a dashboard for the garden where you can control the flow control valves for your garden based on information from the sensors. We will demonstrate this with a simple example and show how you can use it to meet your requirements.

We will make use of the `flask` framework to build our dashboard. If you haven't installed the `flask` framework (from the previous chapters), you can install it as follows:

```
sudo pip3 install flask
```

If you are not familiar with the flask framework, we have written up some basics and getting started in `Chapter 7`, *Requests and Web Frameworks*. We are going to discuss controlling the relay board (shown in the picture here) from a web dashboard (available at h ttp://a.co/1qE0I3U).

Relay module

The relay board consists of eight relays that could be used to control eight devices. The relays are rated for 10A, 125V AC and 10A, 28V DC.

 It is important to follow safety regulations while trying to control AC appliances using a relay board. If you are a beginner in electronics, we recommend using the unit, `http://a.co/9WJtANZ`. It comes with the requisite circuitry and protections (shown in the following figure). **Safety first!**

Enclosed high power relay for Raspberry Pi

Each relay on the 8-relay board consists of the following components: an optocoupler, transistor, relay, and a freewheeling diode (shown in the schematic here):

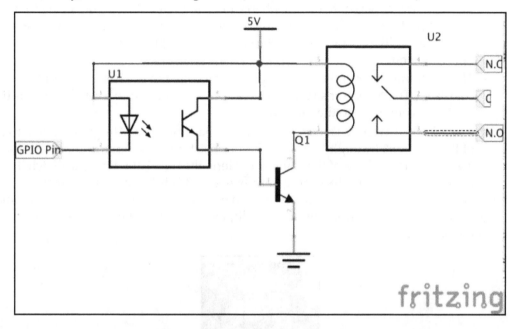

Schematic of one relay on 8-relay board (generated using fritzing)

 The schematic is used to explain the function of the relay board; hence, it is not accurate. It is missing some discrete components.

1. The relay board requires a 5V power supply (through the Vcc pin):

Vcc, GND and GPIO pins

2. Each relay on the relay board is controlled by pins **IN1** through **IN8**. Each pin is connected to an optocoupler (optoisolator-**U1** in the schematic). The function of the isolator is to separate the Raspberry Pi from high voltages connected to the relay. It protects from any transient voltages while switching the relays (we have provided additional resources at the end of this chapter to better understand optocouplers).

3. The phototransistor of the optocoupler is connected to the base of an NPN transistor. The NPN transistor's collector pin is connected to a relay, whereas the emitter is connected to the ground.

4. The relay is driven by an active-low signal that is when a 0V signal is given to one of the pins, **IN1** through **IN8**. The phototransistor (of the optocoupler) sends a *high* signal to the base of the transistor. Here, the transistor acts as a switch. It closes the circuit and thus energizes the relay. This is basically the transistor switching circuit that we discussed in an earlier chapter except for an additional component, the optocoupler. An LED lights up indicating that the relay is energized.

The components of each relay circuit (labeled)

We strongly recommend reading about optocouplers to understand their need and how an active-low signal to this relay board drives the relays.

5. Across each relay, there is a flywheel diode. A flywheel diode protects the circuit from any inductive kickback voltages of the relay when the relay is de-energized/turned off. (We have included a reading resource on relays and inductive kickbacks at the end of this chapter.)

6. Each relay has three terminals, namely the common terminal, normally open terminal, and the normally closed terminal. When an active-low signal is used to drive one of the relays, the common terminal comes into contact with the normally open terminal. When the relay is de-energized, the common terminal comes into contact with the normally closed terminal. Hence, the terminals have the name, normally open and normally closed (The terminals are highlighted with the labels N.O., C, and N.C. in the picture here).

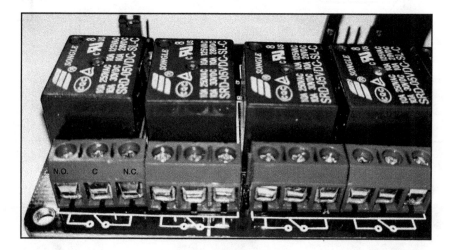

The terminals of a relay

7. The device that needs to be controlled using the web dashboard needs to be connected to the relay terminals, as shown in the schematic given later. For example, let's consider a device that is powered using a 12V adapter. The device's needs to be rigged such that the positive terminal of the power jack is connected to the common terminal of the relay. The normally open terminal is connected to the device's positive line. The device's ground is left untouched. Keep the power adapter plugged in, and the device shouldn't turn on as long as the relay is not energized. Let's review controlling this device using a web dashboard.

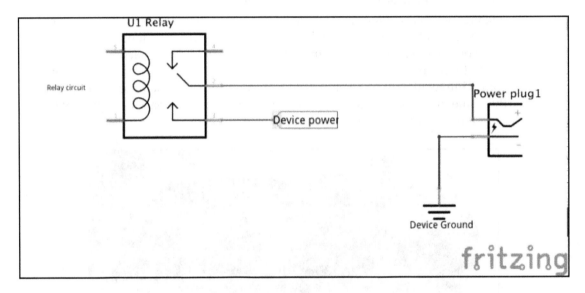

Schematic to rig a 12V DC appliance with a relay

 For an AC power appliance, we recommend using the power switch tail II or the AC relay unit discussed earlier in this section. They are safe for hobby grade applications.

# Building the web dashboard

The first step is creating the html template for the dashboard. Our dashboard is going to enable controlling four appliances, that is, turn them on or off:

1.  In our dashboard, we need an `htmltable` where each row on the table represents a device, as follows:

```
<table>
    <tr>
        <td>
            <input type="checkbox" name="relay"
             value="relay_0">Motor</input> </br>
        </td>
        <td>
            <input type="radio" name="state_0" value="On">On
            </input>
                <input type="radio" name="state_0" value="Off"
                checked="checked">Off</input>
        </td>
    </table>
```

2.  In the preceding code snippet, each device state is encapsulated in a data cell `<td>`,each device is represented by a `checkbox`, and the device state is represented by an on/off `radio` button. For example, a motor is represented as follows:

```
<td>
    <input type="checkbox" name="relay"
    value="relay_0">Motor</input> </br>
</td>
<td>
    <input type="radio" name="state_0" value="On">On
    </input>
    <input type="radio" name="state_0" value="Off"
    checked="checked">Off</input>
</td>
```

On the dashboard, this would be represented as follows:

| | |
|---|---|
| ☐ Motor | ○ On ◉ Off |
| ☐ Tank Light 1 | ○ On ◉ Off |
| ☐ Tank Light 2 | ○ On ◉ Off |
| ☐ Submersible Pump | ○ On ◉ Off |

Device represented by a checkbox and radio button

3. The table is encapsulated in an `html form`:

```
<form action="/energize" method="POST">
    <table>
    .
    .
    .
    </table>
</form>
```

4. The device states are submitted to the `flask` server when the user hits the `energize` button:

```
<input type="submit" value="Energize" class="button">
```

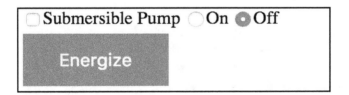

Energize button

5. On the server side, we need to set up the GPIO pins used to control the relays:

```
NUM_APPLIANCES = 4

relay_index = [2, 3, 4, 14]
```

6. The list `relay_index` represents the GPIO pins being used to control the relays.

7. Before starting the server, we need to create an `OutputDevice` object (from the `gpiozero` module) for all the devices:

```
for i in range(NUM_APPLIANCES):
        devices.append(OutputDevice(relay_index[i],
                               active_high=False))
```

8. The `OutputDevice` object meant for each device/relay is initialized and added to the `devices` list.

9. When the form is submitted (by hitting the energize button), the POST request is handled by the `energize()` method.

10. We are controlling four devices that are represented by `relay_x`, and their corresponding states are represented by `state_x`, that is, **On** or **Off**. The default state is **Off**.

11. When a form is submitted by the user, we determine if the POST request contains information related to each device. If a specific device needs to be turned on/off, we call the `on()`/`off()` method of that device's object:

```
relays = request.form.getlist("relay")
for idx in range(0, NUM_APPLIANCES):
    device_name = "relay_" + str(idx)
    if device_name in relays:
        device_state = "state_" + str(idx)
        state = request.form.get(device_state)
        print(state)
        if state == "On":
            print(state)
            devices[idx].on()
        elif state == "Off":
            print(state)
            devices[idx].off()
```

12. In the preceding code snippet, we fetch information related to all relays as a list:

```
relays = request.form.getlist("relay")
```

13. In the form, each device is represented by a value `relay_x` (relay_0 through relay_3). A `for` loop is used to determine a specific relay is turned on/off. The state of each device is represented by the value `state_x` where x corresponds to the device (from 0 through 3).

14. The GPIO pins used in this example are connected to the relay board pins, IN1 through IN4. The relay board is powered by the Raspberry Pi's GPIO power supply. Alternatively, you may power it using an external power supply. (You still need to connect the ground pin of the Raspberry Pi Zero to the relay board.)

15. The earlier-mentioned dashboard is available along with this chapter under the subfolder `flask_framework_appliance` (including the `flask` server, html files, and so on.). In the following snapshot, the **Motor** and **Tank Light 2** are checked and set to **On**. In the picturehere, the first and the third relay are energized.

Turning on Motor and Tank Light 2

Relays 1 and 3 energized

**Exercise for the reader:**

In this section, we made use of a `POST` request to control devices. How would you make use of a `GET` request to display room temperature from a temperature sensor?

**Project ideas/enhancements:**

- With some basic web design skills, you should be able to build a dashboard with better aesthetic appeal.
- Keep in mind that a dashboard should provide as detailed information as possible. Determine how data visualization tools could enhance your dashboard.
- Consider replacing the checkbox and radio buttons with a sliding toggle switch (the type used in mobile applications).
- You can build a dashboard for switching holiday light sequences from your local browser. Think of ways to compete with your neighbours during the holidays.
- You can permanently install the relay board and the Raspberry Pi Zero in a weather proof enclosure as given at `http://www.mcmelectronics.com/product/21-14635`. Check out this book's website for some examples.

# Personal Health Improvement—Sitting is the new smoking

 This project makes use of specific accessories. You are welcome to substitute it with alternatives.

So far, we have discussed projects that could be an enhancement around your living environment. In this section, we are going to write some Python code on the Raspberry Pi Zero and build a tool that helps improving your personal help.

According to the World Health Organization, physical activity of 150 minutes in a week can help you stay healthy. Recent studies have found that walking 10,000 steps in a day can help avoid life style diseases. We have been making use of pedometers to keep track of our daily physical activity. It is difficult to maintain consistency in physical activity as we tend to ignore our personal health over daily commitments. For example, in the physical activity timeline shown here, you will note that all the physical activity is concentrated toward the end of the day.

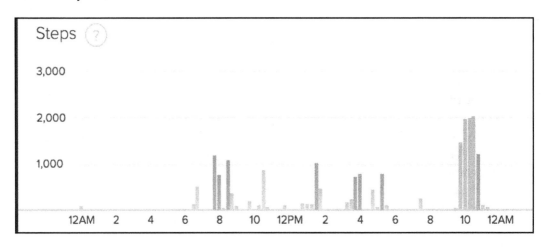

Physical activity in a day (data fetched from a commercially available pedometer)

We are going to build a visual aid that would remind us to stay physically active. We believe that this tool should help put your personal fitness tracker to good use. The following are the recommended accessories for this project:

- **Pedometer**: The cost of pedometers vary anywhere from $20-$100. We recommend getting a tracker from Fitbit since it comes with extensive developer resources. It is not required to have a tracker. We are going to demonstrate this visual aid using a Fitbit One (`http://a.co/8xyNSmg`) and suggest alternatives at the end.

- **Pimoroni Blinkt (optional)**: This is an LED strip (`https://www.adafruit.com/product/3195`) that can be stacked on top of your Raspberry Pi Zero's GPIO pins (shown in the picture here).

Pimoroni Blinkt

- **Pimoroni Rainbow HAT (optional** `https://www.adafruit.com/products/3354`**)**: This is an add-on hardware designed for the Android Things platform on the Raspberry Pi. It comes with LEDs, 14-segment displays, and a buzzer. It can come handy for the project.

Rainbow HAT for android things

- Alternatively, you may add LED strips and components to this visual aid using your creativity.

# Installing requisite software packages

The first step is installing the requisite packages. Because we are going to make use of the Fitbit tracker, we need to install the `fitbit python client`:

```
sudo pip3 install fitbit cherrypy schedule
```

If you are going to make use of the Pimoroni Blinkt LED strip, you should install the following package:

```
sudo apt-get install python3-blinkt
```

If you are going to be making use of the rainbow HAT, the following package needs to be installed:

```
curl -sS https://get.pimoroni.com/rainbowhat | bash
```

# Getting access keys for Fitbit client

We need access keys to make use of the Fitbit API. There is a script available from the fitbit python client repository at `https://github.com/orcasgit/python-fitbit`.

 The access keys can also be obtained from the command-line terminal of a Linux or Mac OS laptop.

1. Create a new app at `https://dev.fitbit.com/apps`:

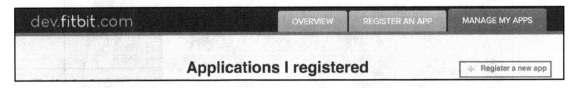

Register a new app at dev.fitbit.com

2. While registering a new application, fill in the description including the name of your application and give a temporary description, organization, website, and so on, and set the **OAuth 2.0 Application Type** to **Personal** and access type to **Read-Only**. Set the callback URL to `http://127.0.0.1:8080`.

**OAuth 2.0 Application Type** *

○ Server   ○ Client   ◉ Personal  ❓

**Callback URL** *

http://127.0.0.1:8080                    ❓

**Default Access Type** *

○ Read & Write   ◉ Read-Only  ❓

✛  Add a subscriber

☐ I have read and agree to the terms of service

Cancel

Set callback URL

3. Once your application is created, copy the **Client ID** and **Client Secret** from application's dashboard.

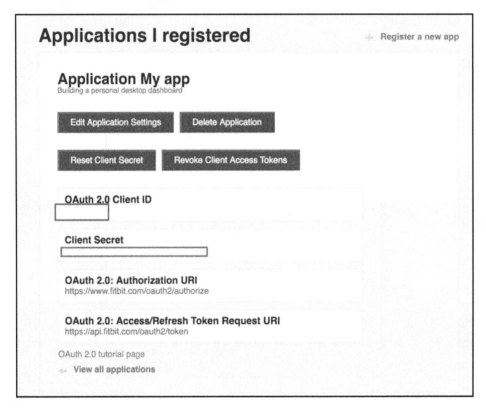

Note down the client_id and client secret

4. From the Raspberry Pi's command-line terminal, download the following script:

```
wget https://raw.githubusercontent.com/orcasgit/
python-fitbit/master/gather_keys_oauth2.py
```

The next step needs to be executed by opening the command-line terminal from your Raspberry Pi Zero's desktop (not via remote access).

5. Execute the script by passing the client id and client secret as arguments:

```
python3 gather_keys_oauth2.py <client_id> <client_secret>
```

6. It should launch a browser on your Raspberry Pi Zero's desktop and direct you to a page on `https://www.fitbit.com/home` requesting your authorization to access your information.

Authorize access to your data

7. If the authorization was successful, it should redirect you to a page where the following information is displayed:

Authorization to access the Fitbit API

8. Close the browser and copy the `refresh_token` and `access_token` information displayed on the command prompt.

Copy access_token and refresh_token

We are ready to use the Fitbit API! Let's test it out!

# Fitbit API Test

The documentation for the Fitbit API is available at `http://python-fitbit.readthedocs.org/`.Let's write a simple example to get today's physical activity:

1. The first step is import the `fitbit` module:

   ```
   import fitbit
   ```

2. We have to initialize the `fitbit` client using the `client key`, `client secret`, `access_token`, and `refresh_token` earlier in this section:

   ```
   fbit_client = fitbit.Fitbit(CONSUMER_KEY,
                               CONSUMER_SECRET,
                               access_token=ACCESS_TOKEN,
                               refresh_token=REFRESH_TOKEN)
   ```

3. According to the Fitbit API documentation, the current day's physical activity can be retrieved using the `intraday_time_series()` method.

4. The required arguments to retrieve the physical activity include the resource that needs to be retrieved; that is, steps, `detail_level`, that is, the smallest time interval for which the given information needs to be retrieved, start times and the end times.

5. The start time is 12:00 a.m. of the current day, and the end time is the current time. We will be making use of the `datetime` module to get the current time. There is a function named `strftime` that gives us the current time in the *hour:minute* format.

 Make sure that your Raspberry Pi Zero's OS time is correctly configured with the local time zone settings.

```
now = datetime.datetime.now()
end_time = now.strftime("%H:%M")
response = fbit_client.intraday_time_series('activities/steps',
    detail_level='15min',
    start_time="00:00",
    end_time=end_time)
```

6. The `fitbit` client returns a dictionary containing the current day's physical activity and intraday activity in 15-minute intervals:

```
print(response['activities-steps'][0]['value'])
```

7. This example is available for download along with this chapter as `fitbit_client.py`. If you have a Fitbit tracker, register an application and test this example for yourself.

# Building the visual aid

Let's build a visual aid where we display the number of steps taken in a given day using an LED strip. The LED strip would light up like a progress bar based on the daily physical activity.

1. The first step is importing the requisite libraries while building the visual aid. This includes the `fitbit` and `blinkt` libraries. We will also import some additional libraries:

```
import blinkt
import datetime
import fitbit
import time
import schedule
```

2. Make sure that you have the requisite tokens discussed earlier in this section:

```
CONSUMER_KEY = "INSERT_KEY"
CONSUMER_SECRET = "INSERT_SECRET"
ACCESS_TOKEN = "INSER_TOKEN"
REFRESH_TOKEN = "INSERT_TOKEN"
```

3. A new `refresh token` is needed every 8 hours. This is a feature of the API's authorization mechanism. Hence, we need a function that gets a new token using the existing token:

```
def refresh_token():
    global REFRESH_TOKEN
    oauth = fitbit.FitbitOauth2Client(client_id=CONSUMER_KEY,
        client_secret=CONSUMER_SECRET,
        refresh_token=REFRESH_TOKEN,
        access_token=ACCESS_TOKEN)
    REFRESH_TOKEN = oauth.refresh_token()
```

4. In the function `refresh_token()`, we are making use of the `FitbitOauth2Client` class to refresh the token. It is important to note that we have made use of the `global` keyword. The `global` keyword helps with modifying the `REFRESH_TOKEN` and enables the use of the new token in other parts of the program. Without the `global` keyword, the changes made to any variable is restricted to the `refresh_token()` function.

In general, it is a bad practice to make use of the `global` keyword. Use it with your best judgement.

5. Next, we need a function to retrieve steps using the `Fitbit` class. We are going to use the same procedure as the previous example. Initialize the `fitbit` class and retrieve the steps using `intraday_time_series`:

```
def get_steps():
    num_steps = 0
    client = fitbit.Fitbit(CONSUMER_KEY,
                           CONSUMER_SECRET,
                           access_token=ACCESS_TOKEN,
                           refresh_token=REFRESH_TOKEN)
    try:
        now = datetime.datetime.now()
        end_time = now.strftime("%H:%M")
        response =
```

```
        client.intraday_time_series('activities/steps',
            detail_level='15min',
            start_time="00:00",
            end_time=end_time)
    except Exception as error:
        print(error)
    else:
        str_steps = response['activities-steps'][0]['value']
        print(str_steps)
        try:
            num_steps = int(str_steps)
        except ValueError:
            pass
    return num_steps
```

6. In the main function, we schedule a timer that refreshes the token every 8 hours using the schedule library (`https://pypi.python.org/pypi/schedule`):

```
schedule.every(8).hours.do(refresh_token)
```

7. We check for the steps every 15 minutes and light up the LEDs accordingly. Because the *Pimoroni Blinkt* consists of eight LEDs, we can light up one LED for every 1250 steps of physical activity:

```
# update steps every 15 minutes
if (time.time() - current_time) > 900:
    current_time  = time.time()
    steps = get_steps()

num_leds = steps // 1250

if num_leds > 8:
    num_leds = 8

for i in range(num_leds):
    blinkt.set_pixel(i, 0, 255, 0)

if num_leds <= 7:
    blinkt.set_pixel(num_leds, 255, 0, 0)
    blinkt.show()
    time.sleep(1)
    blinkt.set_pixel(num_leds, 0, 0, 0)
    blinkt.show()
    time.sleep(1)
```

8. For every multiple of `1250` steps, we set an LED's color to green using the `blinkt.set_pixel()` method. We set the next LED to a blinking red. For example, at the time of writing this section, the total number of steps was 1604. This is (1250 x1) + 354 steps. Hence, we light up one LED in green and the next LED blinks red. This indicates that the steps are in progress.

9. The picture here shows the blinking red LED when the progress was less than `1250` steps:

Physical activity progress less than 1250 steps

10. After walking around, the progress shifted to the right by one LED:

Physical activity at 1604 steps

11. The next step is to set off a buzzer when there is no minimum physical activity. This is achieved by connecting a buzzer to the GPIO pins of the Raspberry Pi Zero. We have demonstrated the use of a buzzer in an earlier chapter.

12. The earlier example is available for download along with this chapter as `visual_aid.py`. We will let you figure out the logic to set off a buzzer when there is no minimum physical activity in a period (for example, an hour).

Install this visual aid somewhere prominent and find out if it motivates you to stay physically active! If you make use of the *Pimoroni Rainbow HAT*, you can display the steps using the 14-segment display.

# Smart lawn sprinkler

In drought-struck states like California, United States, there are severe restrictions on water usage in certain parts of the state. For example: In summer, some cities passed an ordinance restricting water usage to 250 gallons per day. In such states, it is ridiculous to find lawn sprinklers going off the day before the rain. We are going to build a lawn sprinkler controller that only turns on when there is no rain predicted for the next day.

In order to build a smart lawn sprinkler, we need a flow control solenoid valve (for example, `https://www.sparkfun.com/products/10456`). Make sure that the valve can meet the water pressure requirements. This flow control valve can be interfaced to the Raspberry Pi Zero using a transistor switching circuit discussed in earlier chapters or the relay board we discussed earlier in this chapter.

1. We will be making use of *DarkSky API* (`https://darksky.net`) to fetch the weather information. It provides a simple response format that could be used to determine if it was going to rain the next day.

2. Sign up for a free account at the website and get a developer key from the console.

3. According to the API documentation, the local weather information may be obtained as follows:

   ```
   https://api.darksky.net/forecast/[key]/[latitude],[longitude]
   ```

4. The latitude and longitudinal coordinates can be obtained using a simple web search. For example, the request URL for Newark, CA is:

   ```
   URL = ("https://api.darksky.net/forecast/key"
   "/37.8267,-122.4233?exclude=currently,minutely,hourly")
   ```

5. The response includes the `current`, `minutely`, and `hourly` forecasts. They can be excluded using the `exclude` parameter as shown in the preceding URL.

6. Now, we need to turn on the sprinkler only if it is not going to rain the next day. According to the API documentation, the weather forecast is returned as a `Data Point object`. The data points include a field named `icon` that indicates whether it is going to be `clear`, `cloudy`, or `rainy`.

7. Let's write a method `check_weather()` that fetches the weather for the week:

```
def check_weather():
    try:
            response = requests.get(URL)
    except Exception as error:
            print(error)
    else:
            if response.status_code == 200:
                    data = response.json()
                    if data["daily"]["data"][1]["icon"] == "rain":
                            return True
                    else:
                            return False
```

8. If the `GET` request was successful, which can be determined by the status code of the response, the `json` response is decoded using the `json()` method.

9. The next day's weather information is available at `data["daily"]["data"][1]` (Print the response and verify it for yourself).

10. Since the `icon` key provides a machine-readable response, it could be used to turn on the sprinkler. Hence, the `check_weather()` returns `True` if it is going to rain and vice versa.

We will let you figure out interfacing the solenoid valve using the GPIO pins. The earlier code sample is available for download along with this chapter as `lawn_sprinkler.py`.

**Exercise for the reader:**

We are making use of the next day's weather information to turn on the sprinkler. Go through the documentation and modify the code to account for current weather information.

**Project enhancements:**

- How would you go about adding a moisture sensor to the controller?
- How would you interface the sensor to the Raspberry Pi Zero and make use of it in turn on the sprinkler?

# Summary

In this chapter, we reviewed four projects involving the Raspberry Pi Zero (and Python programming) that focused on specific improvements around the house. This includes a voice assistant, web framework-based appliance control, physical activity motivation tool, and a smart lawn sprinkler. The idea behind these projects were to demonstrate the applications of python programming in improving our quality of life. We could demonstrate that it is possible to build applications (using the Raspberry Pi Zero) that can serve as a better alternative to expensive off-the-shelf products.

We also recommend the following project ideas for your consideration:

- **Slack channel-based appliance control**: Are you concerned about the temperature conditions back home for your pets while you are away at work? How about setting up a temperature sensor to send a slack channel alert suggesting that you turn on the air conditioner?
- **Tabletop fountain**: Using a Raspberry Pi Zero and an RGB LED strip, you can create lighting effects for a tabletop fountain.
- **Bird feeder monitor**: This is something we have been working on for a while now. We are trying to track birds that come to feed in a backyard feeder. The bird feeder is equipped with a Raspberry Pi Zero and a camera. Stay tuned to this book's website for some updates.
- **Holiday lights controller**: How about some special light and audio effects during the holidays?

- **Controlling off-the-shelf products using Raspberry Pi Zero**: Do you have a lot of Wi-Fi-enabled electrical outlets lying around unused? Why not try to control them using your Raspberry Pi Zero (hint: *IFTTT*).
- **Pomodoro timer**: Have you heard of the Pomodoro technique for productivity? How about an interactive device to improve your productivity?

### Learning Resources

- **Setting USB Soundcard as the default audio source**:
  http://raspberrypi.stackexchange.com/a/44825/1470
- **arecord/aplay options**:
  http://quicktoots.linux-audio.com/toots/quick-toot-arec
  ord_and_rtmix-1.html
- **MAX9814 setup tutorial**:
  https://learn.adafruit.com/adafruit-agc-electret-microp
  hone-amplifier-max9814/wiring-and-test
- **Understanding optocouplers**:
  https://www.elprocus.com/opto-couplers-types-applicatio
  ns/
- **Relays and kickback voltages**:
  http://www.coilgun.info/theoryinductors/inductivekickba
  ck.htm

# 11
# Tips and Tricks

We have discussed different concepts of Python programming and the applications you could develop in Python using the Raspberry Pi Zero as a platform. Before we call it a day, we would like to present some tips and tricks that could be useful to you. We will also discuss topics that we promised to discuss in this chapter.

## Change your Raspberry Pi's password

As you develop applications, you will gravitate toward buying more than one Raspberry Pi Zero boards. As soon as you finish setting up the micro SD card and power up the board, change the default password for your Raspbian login. Default passwords on connected devices wreaked havoc during **Mirai botnet attacks** of 2016 (`https://blogs.akamai.com/2016/10/620-gbps-attack-post-mortem.html`). Considering the magnitude of the attacks, the Raspberry Pi foundation released a new OS update (`https://www.raspberrypi.org/blog/a-security-update-for-raspbian-pixel/`) that disables SSH access to the Raspberry Pi by default. You can change the password in the following two ways:

- Change it from the desktop. Go to **Menu** | **Preferences** | **Raspberry Pi Configuration**. Under the **System** tab, select **Change Password**.
- Launch the command-line terminal and enter `passwd` at the prompt. It will prompt you for the current password of the Raspberry Pi desktop followed by the new password.

# Updating your OS

From time to time, there might be relevant security updates for the Raspbian OS. Subscribe to updates from the Raspberry Pi foundation's blog to keep yourself informed of such alerts. Whenever there is an update for your OS, it could be updated from the Command Prompt as follows:

```
sudo apt-get update
sudo apt-get dist-upgrade
```

 Sometimes, OS updates can break the stability of some interface drivers. Proceed with caution and check relevant forums for any reports of problems.

# Setting up your development environment

Let's discuss setting up your development environment in order to work on your Raspberry Pi Zero:

1. SSH access to the Raspberry Pi is disabled by default. Launch Raspberry Pi configuration from your desktop. On the top-left corner, Go to **Menu | Preferences | Raspberry Pi Configuration**:

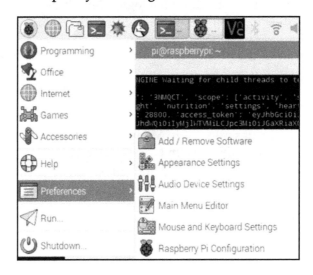

Launch Raspberry Pi configuration

2. Under the **Interfaces** tab of the Raspberry Pi configuration, enable **SSH** and **VNC** and click on **OK** to save changes.

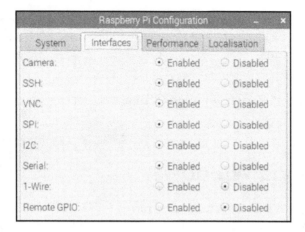

Enable SSH and VNC

3. Launch the Raspberry Pi's Command Prompt and type the following command: `ifconfig`. If you connected your Raspberry Pi Zero to the network using a Wi-Fi adapter, locate the IP address of your Raspberry Pi Zero under `wlan0`, as shown in the following screenshot. In this case, the IP address is `192.168.86.111`:

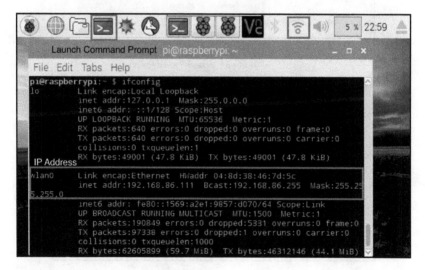

IP address of the Raspberry Pi Zero

4. You can also find the IP address by hovering over the Wi-Fi symbol on the top-right corner.

> The IP address information may not be useful if your network is behind a firewall. For example, public wireless networks, such as a coffee shop, have firewalls.

Now that the Raspberry Pi Zero is set up for SSH access, let's try to gain access to the Raspberry Pi remotely.

# SSH access via Windows

1. If you have a Windows laptop, download **PuTTY** client from (`http://www.chiark.greenend.org.uk/~sgtatham/putty/download.html`). Launch `putty.exe`.

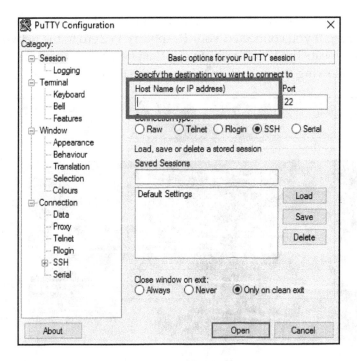

Launch putty.exe

2. Enter the IP address of your Raspberry Pi Zero in the highlighted area and click on **Open**.

3. Select **Yes** if a prompt (like the one shown in the following screenshot) shows up to save the settings:

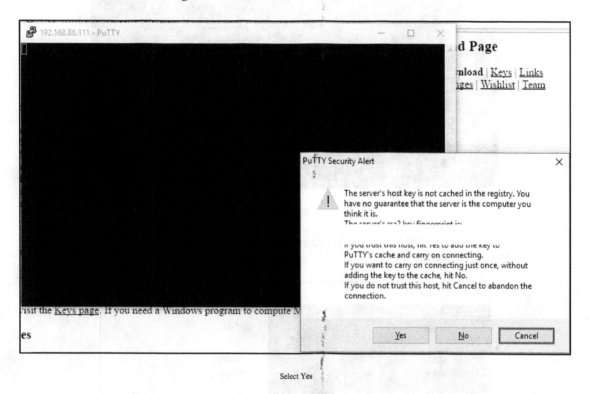

Select Yes

4. Log in as `pi` and enter your Raspberry Pi's password:

Log in as pi

5. You have now gained remote access of your Raspberry Pi. Try executing the commands on your desktop.

```
login as: pi
pi@192.168.86.111's password:

The programs included with the Debian GNU/Linux system are free software;
the exact distribution terms for each program are described in the
individual files in /usr/share/doc/*/copyright.

Debian GNU/Linux comes with ABSOLUTELY NO WARRANTY, to the extent
permitted by applicable law.
Last login: Mon Jan  2 15:07:29 2017 from sais-mbp-29277.lan
pi@raspberrypi:~ $ ls
342718__gadzooks__ting-bounce.wav    gather_keys_oauth2.py        Public
audio_test.py                        houndify_python3_sdk_0.5.0   python_games
beep.wav                             Music                        query.wav
Desktop                              oldconffiles                 speech.sh
Documents                            Pictures                     Templates
Downloads                            Pimoroni                     Videos
pi@raspberrypi:~ $
```

Play with the remote desktop

6. If the PuTTY SSH session disconnects for some reason, right-click and select **Restart Session**.

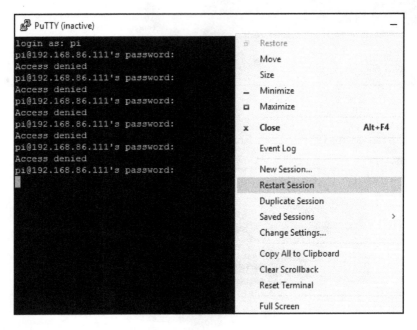

Restart a session with a right-click

# SSH access via Linux/macOS

Perform the following steps for SSH access via Linux/macOS:

1. On a macOS, you can launch the Terminal as follows: Press command + spacebar and launch the search tool. Enter `Terminal` and click on the first option to launch a new Terminal window.

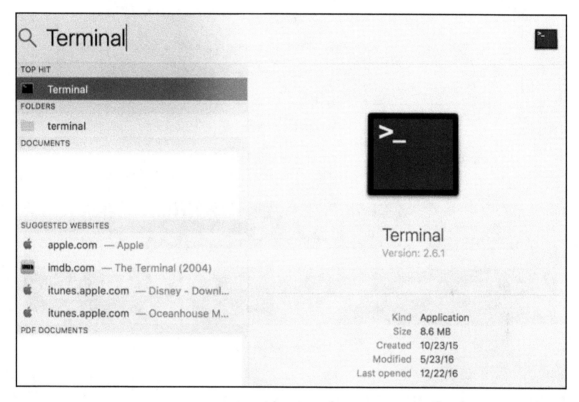

Launch Terminal

2. On the Terminal, log in to your Raspberry Pi using the `ssh` command:

```
ssh pi@192.168.86.111 -p 22
```

3. Enter the password of your Raspberry Pi when prompted and gain remote access to your Raspberry Pi.

```
Last login: Mon Jan  2 17:42:39 on ttys011
[Sais-MBP-29277:~ sai$ ssh pi@192.168.86.111 -p 22
[pi@192.168.86.111's password:

The programs included with the Debian GNU/Linux system are free software;
the exact distribution terms for each program are described in the
individual files in /usr/share/doc/*/copyright.

Debian GNU/Linux comes with ABSOLUTELY NO WARRANTY, to the extent
permitted by applicable law.
Last login: Mon Jan  2 23:58:44 2017 from desktop-7nhn6dm.lan
pi@raspberrypi:~ $
```

Remote access via macOS terminal

4. On an Ubuntu desktop, a Terminal can be launched using the shortcut *Ctrl* + *Alt* + *T* on the keyboard. SSH access is similar to that of macOS.

```
sai@sai-VirtualBox: ~
sai@sai-VirtualBox:~$ ssh pi@192.168.86.111 -p 22
The authenticity of host '192.168.86.111 (192.168.86.111)' can't be established.
ECDS
Are you sure you want to continue connecting (yes/no)? yes
Warning: Permanently added '192.168.86.111' (ECDSA) to the list of known hosts.
pi@192.168.86.111's password:
```

An SSH access via Ubuntu

# Transferring files to/from your Pi

While writing code for your project, it would be easier to write the code on a laptop and transfer the files to the Raspberry Pi to test it remotely. This is helpful, especially while remote access is necessary (for example, the robot in `Chapter 9`, *Let's build a robot!*).

# WinSCP

1. On a Windows machine, WinSCP (`https://winscp.net/eng/index.php`) could be used for files transfers in both directions. Download the software and install it on your laptop.
2. Launch WinSCP and enter the IP address, username, and password of the Raspberry Pi Zero in the window. Under the **File protocol:** drop-down menu, choose **SFTP** or **SCP**.

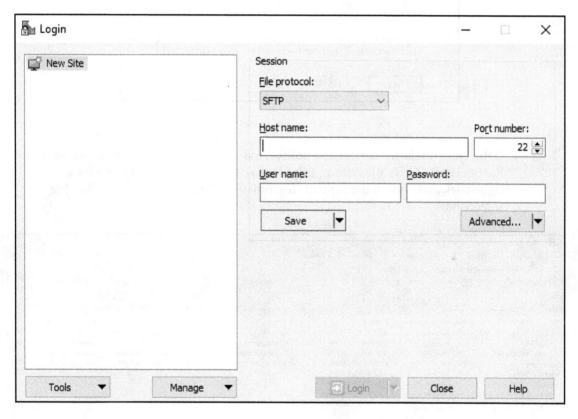

Enter the IP address, username, and password

3. Click on **Yes** when the software prompts whether it is a trusted host:

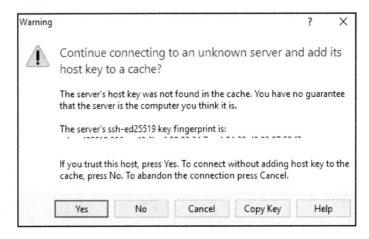

Click on Yes on this warning

4. If the credentials are correct, the software should provide the remote access of the Raspberry Pi Zero's filesystem. In order to download files or upload files, just right-click and choose the upload/download option (shown in the following screenshot):

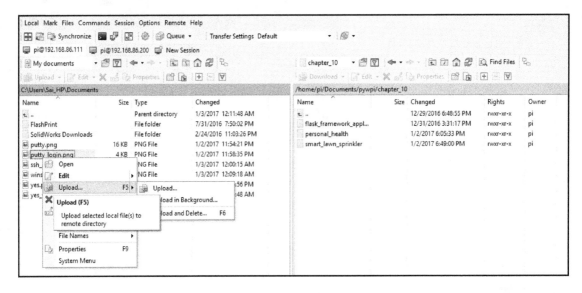

Upload/download files with a right-click

# Mac/Linux environment

In a Mac/Linux OS environment, the `scp` command could be used to transfer files to/from Raspberry Pi. For example, a file could transferred to the Raspberry Pi using the following syntax:

```
scp <filename> pi@<IP address>:<destination>
scp my_file pi@192.168.1.2:/home/pi/Documents
```

A file could be transferred from the Raspberry Pi as follows:

```
scp pi@<IP address>:<file location> <local destination>
scp pi@192.168.1.2:/home/pi/Documents/myfile Documents
```

# Git

Git is a version control tool that can be helpful while developing applications. It also enables sharing code samples with others. For example, this book's latest code samples are all checked into `https://github.com/sai-y/pywpi.git`. Since git enables version control, it is possible to save copies of the code at different stages of the project. It is also possible to revert to a known working version if there are problems in the code.

While writing this book, we wrote our code using text editors, such as *Notepad++* and *Sublime Text editor*. and saved them to our repositories on `github`. On the Raspberry Pi side, we made a copy of the repository from `github` and tested our code. `Git` also enables creating branches, which is a cloned image of the code repository. `Git` branches enable working on a new feature or fix an existing problem without breaking the working version of the code. Once the feature has been implemented or a problem is fixed, we can merge the changes with the main branch of the repository. We recommend finishing this tutorial to understand the importance of `Git`, so refer to `https://guides.github.com/activities/hello-world/`.

# Command-line text editors

From time to time, there might be a need to make minor changes to code files or change configuration files from the command line. It is impractical to use a graphical text editor every time. There are command-line text editors that can come handy with some practice.

One useful text editor that comes with the Raspbian OS is **nano**. nano is a very simple text editor, and it is very easy to use. For example, let's consider a scenario where we would like to add a secret key for an API in your code file. This could be accomplished by opening the file via the Command Prompt (SSH or the command-line terminal from the desktop):

```
nano visual_aid.py
```

It should open the contents of the file, as shown in the following screenshot:

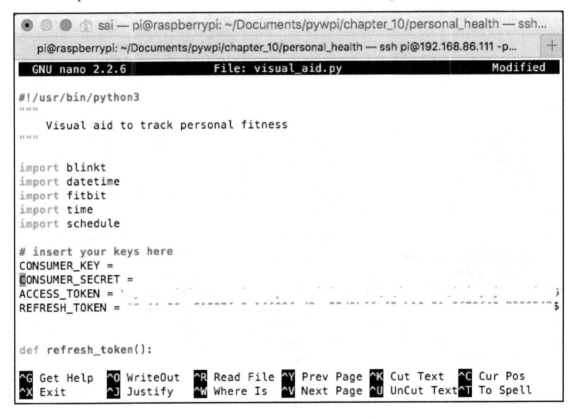

nano text editor

1. Navigate to the line that needs editing using the keyboard's arrow keys. The line could be edited manually, or the secret key could be pasted into the file (CMD + *V* on Mac, *Ctrl* + *Shift* + *V* on Ubuntu Terminal and simply right-click on **PuTTY**).

2. Once the file editing is complete, press *Ctrl* + *X* to finish editing and Press *Y* to save the changes:

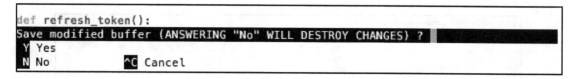

```
def refresh_token():
Save modified buffer (ANSWERING "No" WILL DESTROY CHANGES) ?
 Y  Yes
 N  No                    ^C  Cancel
```

Save changes

3. Press *Enter* at the next prompt to save the contents to the file.

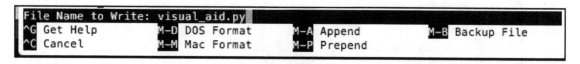

```
File Name to Write: visual_aid.py
^G  Get Help      M-D  DOS Format     M-A  Append        M-B  Backup File
^C  Cancel        M-M  Mac Format     M-P  Prepend
```

Save contents to the original file

Learning to use command-line text editors can come handy while working on projects.

 There are other text editors such as vi and vim. However, nano text editor is much simpler to use.

# Graphical text editors

Apart from IDLE's graphical text editor, there are many other text editors out there. On *Windows*, we recommend using Notepad++ (https://notepad-plus-plus.org/). It comes with a lot of plugins and features that distinguish Python keywords from other parts of the code. It also provides visual aid to indent your code properly.

Notepad++ editor

While Notepad++ is free, there is a cross-platform (there is a version for Windows, Ubuntu, and Mac) text editor named Sublime (https://www.sublimetext.com/) that comes with an evaluation license, but the license costs USD 70. We believe that it is worth the cost because it comes with a rich development environment.

```python
lawn_sprinkler.py    ×
1  #!/usr/bin/python3
2  """
3      Smart Water Sprinkler Example
4  """
5
6  import requests
7  import schedule
8  import time
9
10 URL = ("https://api.darksky.net/forecast/key"
11 "/37.8267,-122.4233?exclude=currently,minutely,hourly")
12
13 def check_weather():
14     try:
15         response = requests.get(URL)
16     except Exception as error:
17         print(error)
18     else:
19         if response.status_code == 200:
20             data = response.json()
21             if data["daily"]["data"][1]["icon"] == "rain":
22                 return True
23             else:
24                 return False
25
26 def turn_on_sprinkler():
27     if not check_weather():
28         # turn on sprinkler
29         print("Turning on sprinkler")
30         time.sleep(600)
31         # turn off sprinkler
32         print("Turning off sprinkler")
33     else:
34         print("Ignoring the sprinker for today")
35
36 def turn_off_sprinkler():
37     pass
38
39 if __name__ == "__main__":
40     schedule.every().day.at("18:50").do(turn_on_sprinkler)
41
42     while True:
43         schedule.run_pending()
44         time.sleep(1)
```

Sublime text editor

# SSH aliases (on Mac/Linux Terminals)

While working on a project, SSH aliases can come handy for the remote access of the Raspberry Pi. An alias is a shortcut for any command. For example, an alias for SSH login can be implemented as follows:

```
nano ~/.bash_aliases
```

Add the following line to the file (make sure that the IP address of the Raspberry Pi is added):

```
alias my_pi='ssh pi@192.168.1.2 -p 2'
```

Load the alias file:

```
source ~/.bash_aliases
```

Now, we can access the pi simply by calling `my_pi` into the Command Prompt. Try it for yourself!

# Saving SSH sessions on PuTTY

In a Windows environment, it is possible to save SSH sessions for repeated usage. Launch Putty, enter the IP address of the Raspberry Pi, and save it with a session name, as shown in the following screenshot:

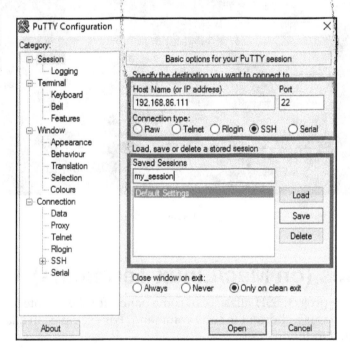

Save session

Whenever the SSH access to the Raspberry Pi is needed, launch PuTTY and load
`my_session` (shown in the following screenshot):

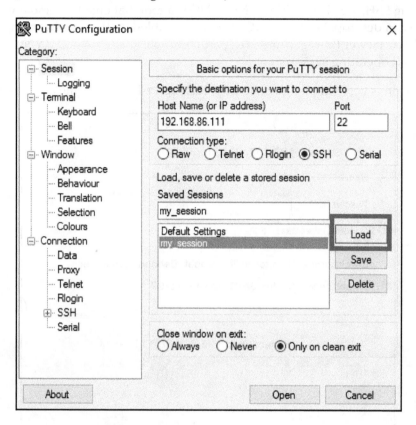

Load session

# VNC access to Raspberry Pi

While enabling SSH, we also enabled VNC. VNC is a tool that enables remote viewing of the Raspberry Pi desktop. Because VNC is already enabled on the Raspberry Pi, download and install VNC viewer (`https://www.realvnc.com/download/viewer/`). VNC viewer is available for all operating systems:

1. Log in is very simple. Just enter the Raspberry Pi's username and password:

| Authentication |
|---|
| VNC Server: 192.168.86.111::5900 |
| Username: pi |
| Password: &#124; |
| ☐ Remember password |
| Catchphrase: Samuel violin acrobat. Baboon Richard lucky. |
| Signature: 8c-56-3b-00-b5-f1-7e-92 |
| Cancel    OK |
| Connecting to 192.168.86.111... |
| Stop |

Login

2. It should take you directly to the Raspberry Pi's desktop.

Raspberry Pi desktop via VNC

# SSH via USB OTG port

This trick is meant for advanced users only.

We came across this nifty trick at
`https://gist.github.com/gbaman/975e2db164b3ca2b51ae11e45e8fd40a`. This is helpful
when you do not have a USB Wi-Fi adapter and a USB OTG converter. We can connect the
Raspberry Pi's USB-OTG port directly to the USB port of a computer (using a micro-USB
cable) and access it via SSH. This is enabled due to the fact that the USB OTG port of the
Raspberry Pi Zero enumerates as a USB-over-Ethernet device when connected to a
computer:

1. Once the micro SD card is flashed with the Raspbian Jessie OS, open the SD card's
   contents and locate the file `config.txt`.
2. At the end of the file, `config.txt`, add the following line to the file:
   `dtoverlay=dwc2`.
3. In the file, `cmdline.txt`, add `modules-load=dwc2,g_ether` after `rootwait`.
   Make sure that each parameter of this file is separated by a single space.
4. Save the file and insert the SD card into your Raspberry Pi Zero.
5. On a command-line terminal, log in using `ssh pi@raspberrypi.local`. This
   should work on Mac/Ubuntu environment. In a Windows environment, Bonjour
   protocol drivers are necessary
   (`https://support.apple.com/kb/DL999?locale=en_US`). In addition, RNDIS
   Ethernet drivers are also necessary
   (`http://developer.toradex.com/knowledge-base/how-to-install-microsoft-`
   `rndis-driver-for-windows-7`).

# The RUN switch of the Raspberry Pi Zero board

The Raspberry Pi Zero has a terminal marked RUN with two pins. This terminal could be
used to reset the Raspberry Pi Zero. This is especially if the Raspberry Pi Zero is installed
some place inaccessible. The Raspberry Pi Zero can be reset by connecting a momentary
push button across the two pins. Because a momentary contact is sufficient to reset the
board, this terminal can be useful where the Raspberry Pi Zero is installed at a very distant
location, and it could reset using an Internet connection (provided that there is another
device that controls the RUN terminal pins).

The location of the Run Pins on the Raspberry Pi Zero

 We also found this excellent tutorial to set up a reset switch for the Raspberry Pi -
`https://blog.adafruit.com/2014/10/10/making-a-reset-switch-for-y`
`our-raspberry-pi-model-b-run-pads-piday-raspberrypi-`
`raspberry_pi/`.

# GPIO pin mapping

For an absolute beginner with the Raspberry Pi Zero, this GPIO mapping plate can be handy. It maps all the GPIO pins of the Raspberry Pi Zero.

GPIO Plate for the Raspberry Pi Zero. Picture source: adafruit.com

It freely fits and sits directly on the top of the GPIO pins, as shown in the picture. The labels can help with prototyping.

## Stackable breadboard

This stackable breadboard is useful to a beginner in electronics. It provides access to all the GPIO pins and a breadboard is sitting right next to it. This can be helpful to quickly prototype circuits for your project needs.

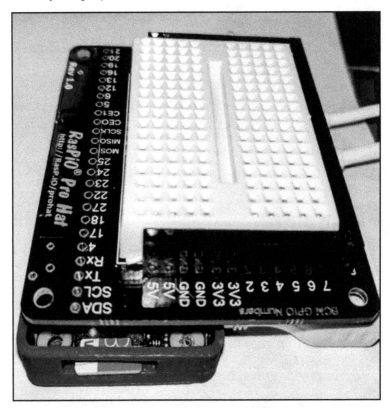

Stackable breadboard

 This breadboard is available at (http://rasp.io/prohat/). We also found another enclosure with breadboard right next to it-http://a.co/dLdxa01.

# Summary

In this chapter, we discussed different tips and tricks to get started with Python programming using the Raspberry Pi Zero. We hope that the content provided in this chapter and all other chapters help you get started.

We wrote this book keeping hands-on practice in mind, and we believe that we have presented the best iteration of our idea. Good luck with your projects!

# Index

www.ingramcontent.com/pod-product-compliance
Lightning Source LLC
Chambersburg PA
CBHW062108050326
40690CB00016B/3250